FINDING YC YLE

SPCK Library of Ministry

FINDING YOUR LEADERSHIP STYLE

A guide for ministers

KEITH LAMDIN

First published in Great Britain in 2012

Society for Promoting Christian Knowledge
36 Causton Street
London SW1P 4ST
www.spckpublishing.co.uk

Copyright © Keith Lamdin 2012

All rights reserved. No part of this book may be reproduced or transmitted in any
form or by any means, electronic or mechanical, including photocopying,
recording, or by any information storage and retrieval system,
without permission in writing from the publisher.

SPCK does not necessarily endorse the individual views contained in its publications.

The author and publisher have made every effort to ensure that the external website
and email addresses included in this book are correct and up to date at the
time of going to press. The author and publisher are not responsible
for the content, quality or continuing accessibility of the sites.

Unless otherwise noted, Scripture quotations are taken from the New Revised Standard
Version of the Bible, Anglicized Edition, copyright © 1989, 1995 by the Division
of Christian Education of the National Council of the Churches of Christ
in the USA. Used by permission. All rights reserved.

The publisher and author acknowledge with thanks permission to reproduce
extracts from the following:
The extract from 'The servant song' by Richard Gillard is copyright © 1977 Scripture
in Song/Maranatha! Music/Music Services (admin by Song Solutions CopyCare,
14 Horsted Square, Uckfield, TN22 1QG, www.songsolutions.org).
The extract from St John of the Cross, 'The living flame of love', is used by permission.
The extract from Eugene Peterson, 'The pain', from Peterson's *The Gift*, is
copyright © 1992 Hodder & Stoughton (www.hodder.co.uk) and Zondervan
(www.zondervan.com) – permission sought.
Every effort has been made to seek permission to use copyright material reproduced
in this book. The publisher apologizes for those cases where permission might
not have been sought and, if notified, will formally seek permission
at the earliest opportunity.

British Library Cataloguing-in-Publication Data
A catalogue record for this book is available from the British Library

ISBN 978–0–281–06478–6
eBook ISBN 978–0–281–06796–1

Typeset by Graphicraft Limited, Hong Kong
First printed in Great Britain by MPG Books
Subsequently digitally printed in Great Britain

Contents

Acknowledgements

I want to thank Ruth, Benedic, Hugo and Zachary, who as close family members have suffered my mistakes with forbearance as well as rejoiced over the small successes that I have managed to make over the years. Ruth has struggled over every impossible sentence of mine and helped me to make more sense than I managed on my own.

I want to thank all my colleagues from Oxford and Sarum College, as well as all those people who invite me to sit with them while they puzzle out something of importance as they lead in their own place. I also want to thank Ruth McCurry, whose confidence in me enabled me to believe I could do this. Without the regular Christmas letters from Robert Gallagher and his willing co-operation in Chapter 8 I do not believe I would have found the inspiration for the idea of the prophet leader.

Without them there would be very little of value here at all. Where this book reveals my mistakes and losses of memory and failures to understand or explain clearly enough there will be no one to blame except me.

An introduction

The world is full of textbooks on leadership and manuals to help you gather a new skill, or to slot yourself into a new way of thinking or working. This book is not another one. This is more of a reflective journey through some of the landscape of leadership and from a distinctly Christian perspective. If there is such a thing as a 'landscape' of leadership then there will be places where the view is good, and I hope that if you are a leader of any kind in a church or congregation you will find it helpful to sit a while with the ideas here and explore the views that they offer you. I hope also that this will help you to understand more easily some of the strains that come your way, and how you might manage yourself when you feel under pressure. I hope too that if you are a Christian working in a range of other 'secular' settings you will find the ideas here helpful in understanding the fashions that hold sway in the world at the moment, and how you as a disciple of Christ might shape your own leading.

From my earliest days I have been interested in how things work, and many of my toys were taken to pieces before trying to put them together again, often without success. As I grew up this passion expanded to take in history, so that I could understand why things are as they are, and psychology, to understand why I was the kind of person I found myself becoming. This soon developed into wondering and exploring how things get done and decisions made. Quite when this became a fascination with leadership I am not sure, but after some years as a Baptist minister in a church I found myself in a training role listening to both individuals and teams and offering them feedback and ideas, which they found useful.

For many years the Church of England Board of Education was a key national player in developing the use of experiential methods of adult education, running workshops of group work, education design and consultancy. This approach was influenced by the foundational theories of John Adair[1] who taught that every group and every leader needs to attend to task, individual needs and the maintenance of the group. It was also shaped by the approach of the American Bethel group work programme, which was adopted and developed by the Grubb Institute[2] and the Tavistock Institute and the Chelmsford Cathedral Centre for Research and Training, which has now closed. The 1970s were a time of a heady mix of experimentation and one of my predecessors here at Salisbury, Harold Wilson, was developing experiential educational methods for ordination training years before it became more generally accepted.

This ragbag of experiences and theories that had come my way was focused when ten years ago I was commissioned by the Bishop of Oxford to gather some colleagues together and develop a leadership training programme for the clergy of the diocese. The course we designed was known as Developing Servant Leaders (DSL) and was adopted by several other Anglican dioceses and a United Reformed Church province. We all learned a great deal about teaching and training leaders. Since coming to Sarum College I have been leading one of our programme areas, which we are calling leadership development, and now teach on our MA in Christian Approaches to Leadership.

While I was still in Oxford, Mike Hill, the Bishop of Buckingham, persuaded me to go to Willow Creek Community Church in Chicago for their annual Leadership Summit, and at that first visit I heard Bill Hybels say some very sensible things. I have gone most years since to this annual event at Willow, even though I do not share much of its theology or its easy and seemingly uncritical baptism of American business methods.[3] However, it is one of the few Christian centres which has given sustained attention to leadership and has sought to embody its thinking in practice. As a living example it is special, and gathers some of the best contemporary thinking about leadership at its annual summit. That first year Bill Hybels had some tips for leaders that have stood me in good stead and I think they inspire the way in which I have approached this small book.

He said:

- Always have a book on leadership on the go.
- Learn from whoever you can, and do not restrict your attention to those who you think you will agree with, or whose theology you approve of.
- Get close to a leader who is ahead of you in the game and learn from him or her without getting in the way.
- Do some leading, if at all possible with colleagues from other disciplines.
- Set yourself some leadership learning goals each year as part of an annual review.

From quite a different world, I remember welcoming a priest from Lesotho who was coming to shadow me in Oxford for several days. I was keen that we should make the most use of the time and asked him what he was most interested in learning and watching. He was very polite but clearly did not understand my language of learning outcomes, intentional learning and success measures. After a while he shook his head and told me about the tradition of medicine men in his part of Africa. He told me that they go out into the wilderness not knowing what they will find, or even if they will find anything. When they do find something and put it in their bag they have no idea when or how they will use it when they get back, or even if it will be useful at all. Some years later I had the privilege of visiting a native African healer in his house and being amazed when he opened his bag for me and spread its contents on his rug.

This rather open-ended approach to learning stood me in good stead for my first visit to South Africa in 1995, when a link was formed between the dioceses of Oxford and Kimberley and Kuruman. There was no way I could predict what I would learn, or which experience would pass me by or influence me for ever. The key was to go and be as open as possible to experience whatever came my way. This was so like much of the early counselling and group work training designed under the mantra of Fritz Perls, who was famous for saying: 'Lose your mind and come to your senses.'

Too much of our educational world at every level is dominated by learning outcomes and measurable results, valuable as they undoubtedly are sometimes. Most of what I have learned has been by experience and chance, integrated by reflective practice. I have also read whatever I can lay my hands on and made my annual visit to Willow to the Leadership Summit.

Inevitably this book is more like a medicine man's bag than anything else and I hope you will use it in any way that works for you. I once heard a speaker on leadership say that there is nothing new to be discovered, only new ways of putting the ideas together. I know that some of the ways I have woven ideas together in this book you will not find anywhere else, and I hope that the way in which I have put ideas together will be useful. Where I have been able to reference something, I have done so, and where I am sure someone else has put it better than I can I have quoted. There have been countless conversations which friends and colleagues will recognize and which I have long forgotten except for the nugget of wisdom that has stayed with me.

There is a structure and purpose to these thoughts that has taken shape over so many years. In Chapters 1 and 2 I take an overview of the ways in which leadership has become an all-encompassing idea, not only in the world but also in the Church, offering my tentative conclusions that leadership is a human characteristic that belongs to all of us and is about seeing what is wrong, and how it could be better, and trying to do something about it.

In the next six chapters I explore different paradigms that I have found operating in church life and examine their content and dynamics. They are monarch, warrior, servant, elder, contemplative and prophet. It is my view that by far the most popular paradigms operating in church today are those of monarch and warrior. They both deliver some real benefits but, I believe, carry within them the seeds and dynamics of dysfunction. The final four are minority paradigms, which I think carry more hope for the Church and for those disciples seeking to offer leadership in the world, beyond the walls of the church building.

In the final chapter I offer some advice for those people who find themselves in leadership positions in the Church where operating out of a monarch paradigm is inevitable and not up for negotiation. My interest here is in providing some ideas about how it is possible to operate and at the same time be aware of the inherent dangers and pitfalls.

If leadership is about influence and change then it is also about power, its use and abuse. Throughout this book I think of power in a number of ways. There is the power you have as a person, with your own body and its strength, and with your own personal history and sense of esteem, which is often thought of as your charisma. I think Jesus will have had a great deal of this kind of power. As you acquire it, this will, over the years, include the power you gain because of your knowledge and skill. There is the power that comes with being appointed to a position. This will include your ability to deploy resources (money and people), to hire and to fire, and to set strategy. Jesus had none of this power at all. There is the power that is called 'projected power', which is given to you by other people, either consciously or unconsciously, and which can be taken away as quickly as it is given. When the crowds followed Jesus he had this, but on the cross, when all his disciples deserted him, he had none of it. Each of these sources of power can be creative and wholesome and each can be malign and unhealthy. Together, to misquote Lord Acton, they have the potential for corruption or for great good.

1

Mapping the territory

I heard recently of a train journey where there was a very extensive delay caused by some mechanical failure. The train was stationary for a long time in the middle of nowhere. Passengers were restless and wanted to know what was wrong. Some of them were missing their connections for the last boat to an island that day, and the temperature of frustration was clearly rising. It was a mechanical fault to some part of the train and engineers were working on it. The tea trolley made frequent journeys up and down the train and the two women staffing it brought solace to everybody.

'Don't worry. I have no idea what is wrong, but we are all in this together and a cup of tea will help.' As the trolley made its journey, the gentle spirit of the trolley staff comforted people and, as they stopped and talked, brought to each part of the carriage a new sense of community and an easing of frustration.

'This was real leadership,' I was told. 'It did not come from those in charge but from these lowly paid trolley assistants.' So what was this leadership? It was not the kind that motivated people to get up out of their chairs and go to the front in an evangelistic rally or 'step up to the plate', as Americans say. Nor was it the kind that painted a future vision that people were prepared to die for. It was something different from those more familiar teachings about leadership, vision and motivation. These trolley assistants read the emotional climate of the passengers on the train and knew that they needed to stay calm and learn how to wait for others to deal with the problem. The two women identified with them, and as well as providing what was to hand – refreshments – in a much deeper sense refreshed them.

On other occasions I have been party to many conversations about the importance of the head teacher to the success of a school, a clergyperson to the well-being of a church, or a bishop to the development of a diocese. There can be no doubt that the person in charge does have a very significant role in any organization.

For example, consider a head teacher appointed to a small rural school. The school had been in the doldrums for some years and parents who had the choice were no longer so keen to send their children there. The loyal and excellent teachers were demoralized and standards were not as high as they should have been. Then some years later the school was performing well, numbers of children attending the school were up and the results were very good. The head quietly went about holding her colleagues to account and raised the demands made upon them, as they had lowered their expectations over the years when they had not been led well. She challenged the children to achieve more, and expected the governors to take responsibility seriously. This was leadership of the kind we are more used to reading about in leadership manuals.

Many years ago I was part of a survey of Anglican clergy in the diocese of Oxford who were leading churches which seemed to be growing numerically at quite a significant rate. There were liberals, evangelicals and Catholics in the mix. The fascinating results were that the only common feature was that each of these clergy followed on from a clergyperson who had not been popular! At the same time it was significant that each of them brought to their particular theological persuasion the same basic skills of relating well, being reliable and trustworthy and leading worship with a sense of presence.

If leadership can encompass these stories, and many more, it is a wide subject and I want now to use a longer example to set out some of the core principles that lie at the heart of any thinking about leadership. More than ten years ago the diocese of Oxford developed and launched a programme of leadership training for its clergy. I want to explain how I think such a programme came about.

Richard Harries had been bishop for a good many years and seemed to have an inner assurance that God would look after the Church whatever was happening in the world. On a number of occasions I heard him talk very positively about the Church. For instance, he stressed that giving had been better than ever; numbers attending church were in decline but not nearly as much as with other national institutions such as trade unions and political parties. Although there was a decline in the number of stipendiary clergy the number of licensed ministers, clergy – stipendiary and non-stipendiary – and readers was as great as at the beginning of the 1900s. This was no time to sound the alarm but to steady the ship.

However, there were others among his senior colleagues who thought that some kind of drastic wake-up call was needed to avoid the looming disappearance of the Anglican Church in England. To use modern churchspeak, they thought that the Church was dominated by a pastoral metaphor and needed to adopt a missional one. They found that the majority of their clergy ministered within that pastoral metaphor, referring to themselves as pastors and teachers rather than as evangelists. Such clergy often see their key role as being leaders of stability and pastoral care, with congregations that need to be cared for rather than challenged. Among these other senior colleagues there was talk about most of the Church being in terminal decline and needing either hospice care or a radical injection of leadership to bring about substantial and lasting change. They wanted a new initiative of teaching and training in leadership.

Bishop Richard was not easily persuaded but I think some statistics about how few people in the country knew anything about Easter changed his mind, and he became increasingly aware of the chasm that was opening up between the Church and most of the people who lived in Britain. He was influenced by the rather vibrant anti-church messages in the media and the more radical atheism that was being propounded. In the end he agreed that something needed to be done.

He called for a major consultation, which started with an invitation to 60 key lay and clergy leaders in the diocese to write a side of paper in response to the question: 'What would the diocese of Oxford look like in ten years' time if it adopted a wholly mission perspective rather than a maintenance one?' These produced a fascinating collection of thoughts which were gathered together and used as a focus for a day's discernment conference. This day and discussions that followed drew out a commitment that the diocese should be:

- centred on God
- orientated towards the world and its needs
- connecting to people, both their communities and their cultures, in new ways
- serious about Christian discipleship.

These were later amplified with some strategic directions, one of which, under the fourth heading, was the priority of training in leadership. It was further established that no 'off the peg' training would do. It had to be focused on the values and practices of change, collaboration and leaders who were first and foremost servants. Each of these values needs a brief explanation.

Change has become a fundamental issue for leadership in both secular and religious texts. I attended a day conference organized on the theme of leadership by the Franklin Covey organization. It started with a video clip of a canoeist in a turbulent river. 'Change is the new constant,' Stephen Covey said.[1] So leaders have to be excellent at handling change, reading it, feeling its energy, discerning where it is taking you, and steering the raft in what Stephen Covey calls our 'white water society'. Bringing about change is much easier to talk about than to do, and there are many books about how to and how not to do it. There is much discussion about the difference between changing the structure of an organization and changing its values or culture. As a planning and training team we used the idea that some people tackle change like engineers who think that something can be taken to pieces, repaired and put back together again. Others behave more like diplomats or politicians who build alliances behind the scenes and push change through when they know they have enough support to win the day. Others prefer to think of themselves as gardeners who are aware of the times and seasons and say they are willing to wait for change to grow naturally; they talk about working organically. Others have adopted the idea of chaos, wave theory and things like social networking and think of themselves as surfers waiting for and catching the waves of change as they sweep in from the deep. Change is not something that can be planned and delivered, they say, but waited for and ridden, or missed.

On the course we taught the theories of Kotter,[2] who identifies eight essential characteristics for any change programme to be successful, and we used the idea of William Bridges[3] that change has to be understood from the psychological perspective of those people faced with the prospect of change. Later on I have found the ideas of Senge, in his book *Presence*,[4] evocative of some of the teaching of the mystics. It may seem obvious that for Christians the religious language of conversion is useful in helping clergy to think about changes they are trying to bring about in their churches.

'Collaboration' is another buzz word that permeates the churches these days. It resonates with the renewed interest in the Trinity as a key doctrine for understanding community and church, and echoes much emphasis in secular leadership texts on the importance of teamwork. This has proved to be very difficult in church contexts. Many clergy, and indeed bishops, have modelled themselves on their vicars or bishops from the past who operated more like a sole trader running a corner shop than a committed member of an organization called a church, diocese, association or province. For them these ideas of collaboration and teamwork have been extremely hard to learn. At the same time the nature of an unhealthy dependency[5] is so prevalent in the churches that the dynamics of desire and hope are projected into church leaders. I deal with the topic of projection and collusion in other parts of the book, and how they make collaboration very difficult as they build distance and separation rather than team and mutuality. I will explore how the ideas of collaboration and teamwork fit with different paradigms of leadership.

We found two writers of great help. Katzenbach[6] identifies the difference between a team and a group, showing that in a real team members actually do depend on each other for both success and failure. They sink or swim together. This helps many Anglican clergy in team ministries to realize that they are not in teams at all but in loose associations of co-workers. We also found helpful the work of Patrick Lencioni, whose *Five Dysfunctions of a Team*[7] is a masterpiece in its clarity and simplicity. If teams cannot focus on results they become embroiled in status and ego. But they cannot achieve this focus until they have found the capacity to hold one another accountable for their behaviour. And they cannot do that until they have committed to the chosen course of action, and they cannot commit until they have argued and tested their differences, and they cannot do that until they have built trust. Very often in church and diocesan teams it is the absence of trust that is reported to me as the key feature that undermines all efforts to build successful teams.

Servanthood is another theme written about by both religious and secular authors. It may seem to stand in opposition to the rather easy quip that you know you are a leader when people follow you, but I shall devote a chapter to this subject and I will argue that a mature understanding of servant leadership should lie at the heart of every person who seeks to be a disciple of Jesus and a leader in the assembly of the faithful, or a Christian leader in other spheres of public life.

Our team shaped a programme around these values hoping that clergy who attended the programme would be more willing to function as leaders of mission rather than maintenance. As we read more and checked with other colleagues developing different programmes, some core principles became clear to me, and I will turn to these in the next chapter. I shall argue in more detail that leaders are very aware of both the best and worst of the organization they belong to and of the world or context in which the organization works, and they know that all is not right. I call this **discontent**, and it is discontent in the heart of anybody that stirs the desire to lead. Knowing that something is not right often brings with it an idea about how it could be better. This is normally known by the word **vision**. The third essential ingredient is the **courage** and resilience to put both discontent and vision into the public arena. These three things, then, call a person into leadership – discontent, vision and courage.

I shall say more about these three things in the next chapter, and for the chapters that follow I have chosen six paradigms that I have noticed leaders in the churches seem to take as their way of explaining and justifying what they do and how they do it. These same paradigms shape the way in which organizations and churches think of themselves and the kind of leader they want. I want to explore their Hebrew and Christian roots. The paradigms are monarch, warrior, prophet, servant, contemplative and elder. I realize that in choosing these titles I have not wanted to use the framework developed by Dulles[8] which has been such a benchmark set of theories about leadership and management in church organization. Nor have I used the metaphors developed by Morgan,[9] which also in their own way have been so important. I have been tempted to go with Simon Western,[10] who suggests that a study of the literature shows a developing series of discourses about leadership from controller through therapist and messiah to a contemporary idea of an eco-leader. All these have influenced me, and those who have already contributed to the discussion inevitably affect whoever writes after them.

Nor have I taken the Pauline set of apostles, evangelists, prophets, pastors and teachers, which has been the base from which Hirsch and Sweet[11] have done such creative work. I am aware that many clergy today think of themselves primarily as pastors and teachers. However, I think these titles are used to describe functions which monarchs, warriors, elders, servants, contemplatives and prophets all do in their own way, rather than paradigms that shape the way they do these things.

I have chosen the idea of these being paradigms rather than just metaphors because they each collect around themselves a set of experiences, beliefs and values that affect the way an individual perceives reality and responds to that perception. In any one leader and church there will be a dominant paradigm. In my early discussions about these ideas some people have suggested that a good leader is able to operate out of all these paradigms and pick and choose, as the context seems to require. This is rather like the idea that we should choose between autocratic, consultative and democratic styles of leadership based on our perception about which would best win the day according to the context and the people we are seeking to lead. As they say, we hope a fireman will not set up a democratic process in the midst of a fire but will tell us what to do.

This kind of 'situational' thinking about leadership has its place but is somewhat superficial. I am reluctant to agree with this pick-and-mix approach and believe rather that any paradigm finds competing paradigms distasteful and impossible to live with. The most obvious example of this, which I shall spell out more clearly in Chapter 5, is that it is impossible to be both a servant and a monarch at the same time. It is possible for a monarch to adopt some of the values of the servant, but to be a true servant one needs to abdicate one's place in the hierarchy.

There is another important perspective to explore, which is the way in which the language we use shapes our expectations. Just for a moment, pause and ask yourself whether you attach any sense of colour or gender to any of these titles – monarch, prophet, servant, warrior, contemplative and elder. When you see the list, do you immediately think to yourself: where are the women or people of colour in this list? Do you naturally see monarch as male or female, black or white? Do you see servant as female first? I have chosen these names for the paradigms specifically because they seem to me to be gender- and race-neutral, or at least ambiguous, so that whatever our colour or gender we can identify with them as we wish. However, I am aware that, as I have shared them with others, some of these titles have evoked a response that they signify more male than female. That is not my intention. It reminds me that we live in a deeply patriarchal society in the West. More often than not this patriarchy has been used and magnified and defended to the hilt in ecclesiastic circles, and in most of our narratives about leadership. One has to look no further than the tortured debates in the Church of England about the ordination of women as bishops to know how deeply ingrained all this is.

But before I turn to the next chapter there are some false beliefs and assumptions that I want to clear out of the way.

The first of these has to do with personality. It certainly helps to know what kind of person you are, what brings you energy and what drains your energy, what situations are easy for you and what kinds are difficult. You may study yourself using the Enneagram or Myers Briggs® or Insights or any other psychometric test, but none of them holds the secret of leadership. To put it simply, leaders come in all shapes and sizes of personality. Character and spirit are a different matter and I shall dwell on these things throughout. You may have some idea that leaders have to be charismatic, have something about their personality that makes them immediately attractive, but all the research into leadership indicates that this is not true.[12]

The second assumption is that leadership is something special. It is not. Let me suggest that we use the word 'leader' to refer to those occasions when a person influences another in some way or other for good or ill. The two boys who took Jamie Bulger by the hand and led him to the railway line, where they killed him, led him there. There may have been manipulation but as far as we know no force. At another extreme we might say that the leadership of Nelson Mandela was expressed in his capacity to influence both friends and enemies. This capacity to influence others is a fundamental human capability, which most of us use much of the time. 'Let's go for a drink after work,' 'Shall we stop for coffee now?' 'I think we should stop flying because of global warming,' are all acts of leadership.

The third is a discussion about whether leaders are born or made or can be trained. I believe we can all be leaders, maybe already are leaders, and we can certainly get better at it if we really want to. I believe that we are all born with this basic human capacity to influence others. If I had not been able to influence my mother from birth with my crying for food I would probably have been dead long ago. However, it is certainly true that individuals do have different gifts or callings in leadership and that naturally some of us make better leaders than others. There can be little doubt that how we have been brought up makes a huge difference to the kind of people we are and the ways in which we find and nourish our gifts. But what I want to stress as strongly as I can is that all of us have natural ability to lead others which we can recognize and nurture, in our response both to the world as we experience it and to our sense of the call of Christ.

Bill George in his book *True North*[13] indicates that leaders who seem to stand head and shoulders above the rest have each had a time in their life that could be described as a crucible experience in which clear insights and passions were burned into their souls and formed them in very definite ways. George tells the story of how Howard Schultz, the founder of Starbucks, was formed in Brooklyn by the experience of having a father who had an accident at work and lived thereafter in abject poverty. Schultz vowed that if ever he had the chance he would ensure that his employees would have health insurance, and whatever we make of Starbucks, it was among the first to provide access to health insurance in the USA for its qualified staff who worked more than 20 hours a week. After hearing Bill George at Willow Creek I have used this learning to help trainee leaders to plot their life story in terms of the crucible experiences they have had. It helps them to discern where and how they have been shaped by the trials and tests of life. For clergy in training the key word used is 'formation', and this seems to be a good word to refer to the ways in which we have come to be the people we are.

So we are all born with the natural capacity to lead. We are all shaped in many ways to find that either we love leading or we hate it. If it seems a gift, we relish using the gift and love learning to be better. We can certainly learn and develop. Warren Bennis[14] states that most of us become leaders only when we take on that role, and uses Shakespeare's *Henry IV Part 2* to show how the young Henry takes on the role of leader as he casts off his friendship with Falstaff.

Building on this idea from Bennis it is worth recognizing that even if we do not feel called to leadership, sometimes it is thrust upon us, and in this we discover new gifts. Sometimes life changes our circumstances and calls us to discover and grow a new area of gifting. I have a friend whose mother became increasingly ill and needed to be looked after. My friend dreaded the prospect but found a new quality of love entering her life as she nursed her mother until she died. She would not have thought of herself as a leader but circumstance required her to discover the role and develop it.

There is a lovely saying: 'It may be possible to train a tortoise to climb trees but it would be better to hire a squirrel.' If you are in the recruiting business you will know how true that saying is, but never forget that a crisis or a disaster or a change in context or circumstance can draw out amazing gifts from people in whom they seem to be completely hidden.

Fourth, it is necessary to have a brief discussion on leadership and management. I do not know where I first heard this but it seemed to make sense to me: 'Leaders work out where to go and managers work out how to get there.' It is also said that all leaders need to know how to manage but not all managers need to know how to lead. It is important to be careful in this rather easy distinction. I recently returned from working with a team where the appointed leader seemed to have all the ideas but had not thought through any of the management implications. This left most of his team members feeling very frustrated. Marcus Buckingham[15] suggests that the key task of a manager is to enable other people to be more productive, and when I think about the responsibility I have to manage myself that seems to make sense. I have to work out all sorts of things about myself that will enable me to be more productive, more useful. So any leader needs to know at least how to manage him- or herself. He or she also needs to understand the issues and implications of strategy and management. And still the leadership question asks: what are you going to be productive for? Where are you going?

Fifth, I have been impressed by how unimportant ecclesiology seems to be. I have worked with Methodists, evangelicals, charismatics, liberals and Catholics who come with many different perspectives and carry all sorts of expectations. Yet in the end they succeed or fail in leadership not because of their theology or their ecclesiology or even how much they pray, but because of their core human capabilities of warmth, wisdom and courage.

Finally, I am often asked whether women lead in different ways from men. Such a question carries a myriad of similar questions about the leadership of people from different cultures. I remember a sentence from a book about the Church and people with disabilities which said that a church without 'disabled' people was itself disabled. In thinking about this question it is possible to start with a negative. Any organization or group – and I include the English Anglican House of Bishops – which restricts its members to only half the population is severely disabled. Without women in senior leadership in all the Church's teams and Houses the leadership of the Church is not only disabled but, I believe, severely compromised. Why should I take notice of anything the House of Bishops says about sexuality when it has been crafted by an exclusive group of men? But it is more complicated to move beyond the negative. There can be no doubt that in different cultures men and women are brought up to see themselves in distinctive ways, and that over time these cultural norms change. While I was brought up with all the traditional post-war stereotypes about what it is to be a man, in recent years such stereotypes have changed beyond recognition. I think it is impossible to find any significant differences between men and women in leadership, even if in the past it may have been true. When I think of the men and women leaders who sit in my room, puzzling over some issue they have to face and thinking about ways of responding, it is the person rather than the gender or the colour or the language spoken that is important, and the solutions different people find do not seem to me to be gendered in any way.

Every book on leadership develops and justifies its own best definition. They all have their value in highlighting a particular facet of leadership. For instance, Clare Huffington[16] identifies the core functions of leadership as vision and strategy, the management of change and the management of boundaries. All these are important and I shall refer to them again when

I look at monarchy. Marcus Buckingham[17] offers a shorter definition and suggests that great leadership is about rallying people to a better future.

There is often a question posed in church circles seeking to establish what is distinctive about 'Christian leadership'. I have come to the conclusion that leadership, like love, is a natural human capacity and that what makes Christian leaders distinctive is their seeking to live as disciples of Jesus. Discipleship informs our discontent, colours and shapes our vision and strategic purpose, and fuels our courage. A Christian leader will always seek to enable people to find and fulfil their God-created potential. But for the moment let the word 'leadership' refer simply to one person's capacity to influence another. In the next chapter I will shape in outline the things that all leaders do, and what defines them as leaders.

2

All leaders do it

With so many definitions of leadership it is hard to know where to start but I am content to go with Marcus Buckingham's definition, mentioned at the end of the last chapter: 'Great leaders rally people to a better future.'

A better future implies both a real awareness of the present and also a realistic idea of a possible future. Peter Senge[1] also emphasizes that leadership has to hold the tension between the present reality and the future that is hoped for. For me there are three essential ingredients to this process of leadership – discontent, vision and courage.

Discontent

I have briefly described in the previous chapter the growing awareness in Richard Harries when he was Bishop of Oxford that the settled relationship between the Church of England and contemporary society was no longer sustainable and was under considerable strain. Research regularly indicated that fewer and fewer people could use the Christian metaphors, liturgies and festivals to make sense of their lives. The gap between what went on in church and what went on in the world was growing larger and larger.

This growing awareness that things are not right becomes one of the essential building blocks for any leader. Bill Hybels, the founder of the Willow Creek Community Church in Chicago, tells of his growing awareness that he would never be able to persuade any of his friends to come with him to the church he went to with his family. It was out of that discontent that he started the new church with some friends. It has been that same sense that produces the energy for what we have come to know as Fresh Expressions of church. Such discontent either breeds despair that nothing can ever be done or brings to birth some kind of vision about how it could be better.

Discontent is a normal human experience and can express itself in any number of ways. We can be discontented with our status in life, or our wealth or lack of it, or our health, or the behaviour of our neighbours, or our body shape, or our gender or the colour of our skin, and so on. We can be discontented with the world, the nation, the Church, our place of work, our marriage and relationships, and so on. The list can be endless.

There is, however, a religious idea that suggests that we should learn to be content with our lot. A verse from a now edited hymn, 'All things bright and beautiful', said:

> The rich man in his castle,
> The poor man at his gate,
> God made them high or lowly
> And ordered their estate.

We probably find that offensive, but there is a similar theme in a popular children's book based on a Jewish European folk tale about a woman who lived on her own and complained that her house was too small. A wise man suggested she should take her animals one by one to live in the house with her, until there really was no room. The wise man then told her to remove each of the animals in turn, and the woman found contentment in the house just as it had been before she began complaining.

Seeking to discern whether a discontent comes from God or from our own misconstrued desires involves a lifetime's work of prayer and discipleship. There seem to be several main dangers for the Christian.

By way of an example, there has been in recent years an increasing interest in personal fulfilment and spiritual growth.

Many retreat centres are reporting having full houses on guided retreats and a range of spiritual conferences and workshops. These things cost money and most of the people there can afford to pay. They also have the time to spend. And they are motivated by their discontent with the quality and depth of their lives. They are searching for something that their life so far has failed to provide. And here's the discernment question: how do these retreat-goers decide whether they are genuine seekers after God and God's will or attempting to fill another self-centred consumer-driven void? In my early days as a spiritual accompanier I was given this set of tests: is this person's narrative and journey bringing him or her closer to God and is it also bringing God's justice to the world?

There are two other kinds of discontent that are not of God. The first is the discontent that arises from an unrecognized desire for power and status. New clergy when they get together often talk about how quickly they are going to bring changes to the church they have been called to. There are two theories. The first is to push through change as soon as possible and the second is to get to know the people and promise to do nothing for the first six months. The issue is not really which is the better strategy but whether or not they have enough self-awareness to recognize some of their own needs and desires that will be expressed in this significant transition period. I reckon that most of the troubles between curates and training incumbents in the Church of England arise from an unrecognized or unacknowledged search for self-esteem through power.

The second is less easy to spot and probably lies deeper in the unconscious process of the human heart. Robin Skynner,[2] famous for his book with John Cleese on *Families and How to Survive Them*, worked a great deal with staff in the caring professions. He noticed that many people who worked in social and health care had not themselves had happy childhoods, and he discovered a pattern in their care. It can be summarized briefly as: 'I had an unhappy childhood and I know how it could have been so much better. I really do understand the nature of love and care. So I am going to find work in which I can bring to others what I myself missed. Yet in doing this I see my clients experiencing what I myself missed and I begin to be envious of them. Then I grow to hate them for what they have that I never did. I know I cannot express my hatred for these needy people so I will create institutions for them to live in that are hateful and I will bring my hatred and dissatisfaction to the institution that employs me so that I can be resentful of my managers.'

It is a pattern repeated in family life. We all know parents who wish they had learned to play the piano as children and who now require it of their children. This kind of love is twisted. In his professional career Robin Skynner found that the only way to help was to provide the kind of supportive casework sessions that offered care not for the clients but for the workers. Then they could begin to understand their distorted processes and find the healing that they needed for themselves.

For a Christian the discontent needs to be based on the teaching of Jesus. This allows us to discover those things about which we must learn to be content and those things which should arouse our discontent. It helps us to know ourselves as loved by God, and thus able to explore all the dark corners of our desires and brokenness.

Vision

According to many leadership theories, what defines a leader is his or her capacity to find, receive, clarify and declare a new future for the organization. Such discernment may come about through many methods. Appointed leaders may consult widely or engage in democratic processes. They may themselves be the bearer of vision or rely on a gifted or inspired associate.

But, so the theories go, in the end it is the leader's task to craft the vision and explain it and keep it ever before the minds of those with whom the leader works. In a less structured organization, anybody can declare a vision for the future and see who joins in. They say in the company that makes Gore-Tex that you know you are a leader when you call a meeting to discuss an issue and people turn up!

In my experience vision is often misunderstood and misused, and my evidence for this is the great number of long vision statements in the vestibules of churches, long forgotten and never used.

There are two very differing attempts at inspiring action by creating a vision in Shakespeare's *Henry V*.

First of all there is the speech to the troops before the battle.

> Once more unto the breach, dear friends, once more;
> Or close the wall up with our English dead!
> In peace there's nothing so becomes a man
> As modest stillness and humility:
> But when the blast of war blows in our ears,
> Then imitate the action of the tiger;
> Stiffen the sinews, summon up the blood,
> Disguise fair nature with hard-favour'd rage . . .
> Cry 'God for Harry, England, and Saint George!'

I remember seeing Laurence Olivier in the film of *Henry V* when I was a child and feeling stirred beyond belief by these rousing words. But Shakespeare knows better, and immediately after this speech sets a short scene with Nym, Bardolph, Pistol and Boy, with a closing thought from the Boy: 'Would that I were in an alehouse in London! I would give all my fame for a pot of ale and safety.' Henry's speech has fallen on deaf ears and in terms of vision it has not worked.

On the other hand, listen to the speech a few scenes later after Henry in disguise has taken a night-time walk among his troops.

This day is call'd the feast of Crispian.
He that outlives this day, and comes safe home,
Will stand a tip-toe when this day is nam'd,
And rouse him at the name of Crispian.
He that shall live this day, and see old age,
Will yearly on the vigil feast his neighbours,
And say 'To-morrow is Saint Crispian.'
Then will he strip his sleeve and show his scars,
And say 'These wounds I had on Crispian's day.'

This speech has quite a different feel to it and paints a picture of the future, when all the warring is over and they are all back in England. It has a similar feel to the famous vision speech of Martin Luther King.

I have a dream that one day this nation will rise up and live out the true meaning of its creed: 'We hold these truths to be self-evident: that all men are created equal.'

I have a dream that one day on the red hills of Georgia the sons of former slaves and the sons of former slave owners will be able to sit down together at the table of brotherhood.

I have a dream that one day even the state of Mississippi, a state sweltering with the heat of injustice, sweltering with the heat of oppression, will be transformed into an oasis of freedom and justice.

I have a dream that my four little children will one day live in a nation where they will not be judged by the colour of their skin but by the content of their character.

I have a dream today.

I have a dream that one day, down in Alabama, with its vicious racists, with its governor having his lips dripping with the words of interposition and nullification; one day right there in Alabama, little black boys and black girls will be able to join hands with little white boys and white girls as sisters and brothers.

I have a dream today.

I have a dream that one day every valley shall be exalted, every hill and mountain shall be made low, the rough places will be made plain, and the crooked places will be made straight, and the glory of the Lord shall be revealed, and all flesh shall see it together.[3]

King's speech ends with words from Isaiah, another writer famous also for his ability to paint word pictures of a future state that warm our heart and evoke our longing. In biblical times people did not have to struggle to engineer vision, as it was given to them in dreams or in 'visions'. We find them mainly in the prophetic books and in the apocalyptic texts, and in the sayings of Jesus himself.

I have come to the view that for all Christians in all parts of the world and in all stages of history the vision is fundamentally the same. It is a picture of a world in which God's will is done and human society is ordered by love (Revelation 21.1–7, 22–27). That is not to say that it does not need re-crafting in language and images that speak to each generation and context.

In his response to his discontent, the Bishop of Oxford led a process of consultation, which produced a vision which was called Sharing Life. He crafted some words:

The new life we have received in Christ is true, authentic existence. It is a life with God that death cannot destroy. It is also life with one another. For *Jesus came to reconstitute human society around himself, under the reign of God*, so the Church is nothing less than a sign of what one day will be the reality for all people. The Christian faith commits us therefore to the transformation of both individuals and communities, beginning with ourselves and the Church and *being satisfied with nothing less than the transformation of the whole of human society*.

I have italicized the parts that at the time for me worked as an inspiration. The words are not very pictorial, nor are they painting a picture of the future, but they do demonstrate something all-encompassing. The diocese of Bristol drew a more explicit future-oriented picture, which I think both picks up the eternal longing of God and brings it into focus:

The year is 2015. In communities across Swindon, North Wiltshire, South Gloucestershire and Bristol, people have been sensing a change.

They are noticing friends, family members or colleagues living differently – in their integrity and generosity, compassion and service. The marginalized and poorer members of their community are being cared for. Faith and community groups are working together with other organizations to address problems in society. There is a renewed concern for the wider world, the environment and social justice. And churches are not only attracting new members but gaining a reputation of meaning and purpose where all ages and kinds of people can come to know Jesus Christ as Lord.[4]

I have increasingly come to the view that vision that is eternal is not enough on its own. We need something else to root us in our context and give us something to grasp here and now. So the big vision needs to be worked out in the small context of where we find ourselves. It needs to be specific and contextual.

This is where the hard work comes in. This is where churches need to discuss and pray and argue until they can find some clarity about their specific contribution, in their particular place, in the time they find themselves. Jim Collins[5] asks of any company: 'What are you passionate about? And what can you be the best at in the world?' This is not a competitive question, as is made clear when it is matched by: 'Who would notice if you closed down and what would the world be missing?' In his monograph *Good to Great in the Social Sectors* he has some wonderful examples of not-for-profit organizations having visions and strategic purpose.

We asked these questions when I came to Sarum College. We quickly answered that we were passionate about hospitality and about learning. We became more specific and said that we were passionate about learning that nourished the human spirit. In a further discussion we became clear that our location in the Close at Salisbury within the shadow of the cathedral brought us a significant context. We knew we offered something distinctive that we thought was worth preserving at all costs. This then is our vision, which we have not crafted as a future story of people's experience of coming here and learning here, although we could have shaped it in that form: 'To be a place where people can find hospitality and teaching that will both nourish their spirits.'

This local vision for Sarum inspires those of us who work here. But we also hope that many of the people who come find something here that nourishes them.

But vision is not enough on its own. It needs to be coupled with something I call strategic purpose. Vision is the picture of the future, and strategic purpose is the careful planning of how to reach it. Vision inspires us and strategic purpose motivates us as we can see that it is possible, step by step, to make progress. Some of my colleagues have much preferred the word 'mission' to express this focused intent, but I prefer the word 'purpose', because 'mission' is so over-used and people so easily muddle up 'vision' and 'mission' and use the words interchangeably. Because of this muddle, most vision or mission statements that I read at the back of churches lose the capacity both to inspire and to motivate. Most mission statements that I read on company walls seem to fail in exactly the same way.

We need something to motivate us, to bind us together in common purpose. The question to ask of any Christian or church goes something like this: 'Given that you long for God's rule of love to shape everything that happens in our world, what in particular is your part, your distinctive contribution, to bring this about?'

It is the strategic purpose that shapes strategy, that gives us a sense of how well we are doing and what we need to do to improve. At Sarum we have honed these purposes down to three: to break even financially so that we can continue to stay in existence; to provide hospitality that people will never forget; and to deliver education that nourishes the human spirit. It is this combination of vision and purpose that inspires and motivates us. It is our purpose that enables us to take tough decisions about our life together and acts as a rudder to keep us on course.

In Oxford the vision was the anvil on which was hammered a purpose statement: 'Our purpose is to create a caring, sustainable and growing Christian presence in the Diocese of Oxford.' This purpose was developed into four strategic directions – centred on God, orientated towards the world and its needs, connecting to people (both their communities and their culture) in new ways, and serious about Christian discipleship.

In Bristol their vision was accompanied by a strategy statement called *Releasing the Energy*, and focused strategic intent on four areas: growth, leadership, structures for support, and income generation.

It is vision and purpose held together but kept separate that makes sense of the comment of Thomas Merton: 'If you want to know who I am do not ask me where I live or what I do, but rather ask me what I am living for, and ask me in very small particulars why I am doing so little about it.'

And this brings me to the third essential aspect of leadership – courage.

Courage

It is all very well being discontented and having vision for the future, but as long as you say nothing and do nothing you are no leader.

Courage is a quality that Aristotle and Aquinas both thought about and is a topic that has been taken up by those who have focused on virtue ethics. At the time of writing, our television news has regularly featured British soldiers who have been killed in Afghanistan. Among the stories are those of real courage and bravery, where soldiers, with little regard for their own safety, put the needs of a colleague before their own and pay the price with their life.

However, there is nothing reckless in courage. A courageous person will see the greater good, carefully balance the risks, stay in touch with his or her own fear and make a decision to act.[6]

The opposite of courage is fear, and I know a number of leaders who appear to be more frightened than courageous. We are living in times when religion is more visible and public in the affairs of the world, and more extreme as well. It has been easy to fear that contemporary disputes will split the Church. Homosexuality divides Anglicans across the world and across generations. Attitudes relating to the episcopal leadership of women have driven a few English Anglicans into the arms of the Ordinariate, set up by the Pope. Larger churches are flexing their muscles and threatening not to contribute to the common purse. Church leaders talk much about being the holders of unity and peace, but in reality seem to be so frightened that some other dispute will wreck the unity of the Church that they give the impression of spending all their time looking over their shoulder.

The problem with fear is that it diminishes the soul and belittles the person, as well as stunting the potential for growth in the organization. Years ago I was in pastoral leadership where the Boys' Brigade believed its importance meant it could not be held to account for the behaviour of some of its officers. The risk was that the BB would leave and that the church would be so weakened that it would collapse. I was a young leader and half believed their threat. The success of the church was important to me and I tried to hold the growing church and the 'badly behaved' BB together. My successor was more experienced and faced a more explicit showdown. The BB left the church, which, rather than failing, grew and went from strength to strength. This is very similar to reported comments from churches where people have left to join the Ordinariate:

'That has been a breath of fresh air,' says churchgoer Ruth Willis . . . 'The congregation is not as big as it was and what it's meant is that we've all had to step into the breach. But everyone is very enthusiastic. It binds us together.'[7]

An aspect of this fear is the imagination of it going wrong. I imagined that if I stood up and held a line and the BB left, the church might in fact fail and my career as a minister might be in tatters. It is the same fear that simmers in the heart of everybody who has been a whistleblower – what is the worst that can happen? And can I take the risk?

Jim Collins[8] develops a schema for five levels of leadership. The first is a highly capable individual, who makes productive contributions through talent, knowledge, skills and good work habits. The second is a contributing team member, who can contribute to group objectives and can work effectively with others. The third is a competent manager, who can organize people and resources towards the effective pursuit of predetermined objectives. Level four leaders can catalyse commitment to and vigorous pursuit of a clear and compelling vision. The level five leaders build enduring greatness through a paradoxical blend of personal humility and professional will. It is this characteristic of professional will that most closely resembles this quality of courage, the ability to know what is right and hold the line steadily and firmly, despite all the things that others may threaten and throw at you.

So in concluding this chapter my premise is that wherever you are and whatever leadership position you hold, these three things define you as a leader. You can sense what is wrong, you can find an inspiring picture of how it could be better, and you can find your voice and speak it out and see who will come with you to make a better future.

3

The monarch

Kings shall be your foster-fathers
and their queens your nursing-mothers.   (Isaiah 49.23)

It should not be surprising that most of the books on leadership come from the world of business, where hierarchy is alive and well. Many of the consultants and university business schools serve this same context, and despite some anxiety about selling their souls to the devil of success and money, many in the Church find the ideas and models of leadership found there helpful.

In a fascinating study John Micklethwait and Adrian Wooldridge[1] plot differences between Christianity and modernity in Europe and the USA. They suggest that modernity in Europe, with its emphasis on rational thought and scientific research, has always been suspicious of all faiths, and in particular Christianity. They suggest that this is because Christianity and the Church had in the past been established with power and control, and had been an organ of suppression by emperors and monarchs. On the other hand, in the USA the same kind of rampant atheism has never been present, and with the disestablishment of religion in the Declaration of Independence faith and faiths of all kinds were tolerated in the private and personal spheres. This has given faith a freedom in the marketplace. Free of state control, Christianity has been able to flourish in a competitive environment, and each of the four 'great awakenings' has adapted and adopted commercial and business competitive processes. It is not surprising to find in a good deal of the American literature significant transferring from the world of business and corporate leadership into church contexts.

Indeed, the development of Willow Creek Community Church has become a standard Harvard Business School case study.

Despite different development pathways in Europe and the USA, the structures, patterns and languages of European monarchy and US corporations seem very similar and in this chapter I use the words 'monarchy' and 'hierarchy' interchangeably. Not many chief executives would call themselves the monarch, but the dynamics of their power is very similar. Nor do I want to make comparisons between all those systems in place in some countries to limit the power of the monarch. These may be democratic practices or annual meetings or government laws. The critical question that reveals that monarchy is alive and well in all sorts of places is the answer to the question: 'Who is in charge?' If at the end of any chain of command there is just one person, then monarchy, whatever it may call itself, is the best way of thinking about it.

There is something simple and direct about hierarchy. The organization has a chart which shows who is in charge of what and how accountability works. The more senior manager gives instructions and the more junior carries them out. If there is a major fault or failure then the person at the top takes the blame, as the Gulf disaster for BP has amply demonstrated. In a properly ordered hierarchical organization you know your place and the freedom and the limits to your authority. If there is a dispute between colleagues, you know who to go to for arbitration or for an executive decision. You know where the buck stops, to use Harry S. Truman's famous phrase that he had displayed in the Oval Office. Pay is related to the amount of power you have and the ladder of success is clearly marked. All priests will know that monarchy is alive and well in the Church of England and only need to remember the words they say before their ordination or at their installation: 'I swear by Almighty God that I will pay true and Canonical Obedience to the Lord Bishop of . . . and his Successors in all things lawful and honest.'

Maybe I could pause a moment and reflect about priestly leadership. William Countryman[2] suggests that all priests are called to walk alongside others in the territory of the holy. There is nothing hierarchical about that, although there is always the possibility of an abuse of power. The moment, however, that a priest is appointed and installed as a rector, vicar or priest in charge, he or she is bound into the hierarchy. Those of us who have spent most of our priestly ministry as assistants and associates have had the rare privilege of being priestly without having the structures of position power hung around our neck. We have had to respond to projected power when people treat us as if we know far more than we do, but the absence of position power makes a real difference. It is not unusual to hear retired priests rejoicing in their freedom to be priests without having to be 'in charge'.

However, at their best, hierarchical organizations are straightforward and the capacity to be decisive is clear. Things can and do get done, and there will always be situations and contexts when it is easy to see how hierarchy works so well. But monarchs and chief executives and bishops soon realize that life in the top seat is anything but straightforward. Many of the books and training courses about leadership are there to help a person in an appointed position of leadership to develop the wisdom and skill to be more effective and efficient in that position. It does not matter much whether the power is given through proper channels or just taken. Being in a senior leadership position is such a difficult work and a precarious position.

Much of the literature is written with the assumption that leaders are those people appointed to positions of power in their organization. It is probable that most of the readers of these books are in such positions and both want to make a better job of it and hope to survive the stresses they experience in the role.

A survey of the literature makes clear the skills appointed leaders are expected to have. They need to be good communicators of reality and vision. They need to have strategic and financial sense. They need to be good at delegating and prioritizing their own workload. They need to run meetings well, be decisive, work well with colleagues and direct reports. More recently, leadership thinking[3] has focused on character as well as skill. Leaders need to be trustworthy, and have ethical sense. They need to be determined and resilient. So the list gets longer and longer, and in today's increasingly uncertain world, as demonstrated by the demands on football managers, the expectations get higher and higher.

I have spent most of my life working in a hierarchical organization in positions of leadership: as a director of a diocesan department, as a priest in charge and now as the principal of Sarum College. I have studied leadership in order to be as good a leader as I can. I have worked closely with bishops and have been a consultant to people who have hierarchical positions, both clergy and others.

There can be no doubt that the person appointed to a position has the capacity to bless the organization or damage it, and the higher up the hierarchy the greater the power to bless or damage. It is impossible to escape the conclusion that the head teacher or vicar or bishop or leader you appoint will have a very significant impact for good or ill. Jim Collins[4] came reluctantly to the conclusion that great companies had great leaders. By that he did not mean that they were famous or even had charismatic personalities, but that they were people who combined some special characteristics of courage and humility. So, whether we like it or not, the more senior we are in any organization the more important our behaviour as a leader will be, and the greater the impact it will have on those who work with us.

That said, there are deep and unavoidable flaws in any idea of hierarchy which need to be explored. Without some understanding of them, all hierarchical leaders will struggle to survive, and many will not do so.

The Hebrew people did not have kings in the beginning, and Samuel did his best to persuade them that trusting in hierarchy was a foolish thing to do. But in the end they chose to have kings – Saul, David, Solomon and the rest. The first book of Samuel chapter 8 has discussions between Samuel and God and between Samuel and the people. The people ask for a king because the sons of Samuel are proving to be very poor judges. Samuel feels rejected, and in a discussion with God hears God say that it is not Samuel who is rejected by this request but God himself. God tells Samuel to give the people a good warning, and he does so. It is worth quoting in full:

> 'These will be the ways of the king who will reign over you: he will take your sons and appoint them to his chariots and to be his horsemen, and to run before his chariots; and he will appoint for himself commanders of thousands and commanders of fifties, and some to plough his ground and to reap his harvest, and to make his implements of war and the equipment of his chariots. He will take your daughters to be perfumers and cooks and bakers. He will take the best of your fields and vineyards and olive orchards and give them to his courtiers. He will take one-tenth of your grain and of your vineyards and give it to his officers and his courtiers. He will take your male and female slaves, and the best of your cattle and donkeys, and put them to his work. He will take one-tenth of your flocks, and you shall be his slaves. And in that day you will cry out because of your king, whom you have chosen for yourselves; but the LORD will not answer you in that day.' (1 Sam. 8.11–18)

The people reply: 'No! but we are determined to have a king over us, so that we also may be like other nations, and that our king may govern us and go out before us and fight our battles' (1 Sam. 8.19–20).

This is the endless psychological contract about power that lies at the heart of all hierarchical constructions of human interaction and community – the desire to be safe and protected from our deepest anxieties. Because it echoes our earliest memories of being looked after, the unconscious contract of dependency that lies at the heart of monarchy is very strong. It is expressed in the dialogue with Samuel as the need to have someone to fight for us. In order to be safe in this way we are willing to give up our freedom, our power and our autonomy.

The mimetic theories of René Girard[5] explore this desire to 'be like other nations', and Iain McGilchrist[6] develops the idea of the importance of imitation in human and cultural development from quite a different perspective. Imitation is not only a natural human ability but, Girard argues, it also fosters desire. I want to be like you because I see something in you that I like and want to have for myself. But such desire also feeds envy and competition and in the end violence, the violence that finds its satisfaction in the death of the scapegoat. Girard argues that such violence deep in our own psyche and in the psyche of human tribes, communities and nations is so frightening that we have developed religious practices and organizational life to manage them. One of the most stable and omnipresent yet problematic strategies seems to be all sorts of hierarchy, as an unconscious contract of containment – monarchy, chief executives, principals, presidents, bishops, prime ministers, managing directors, and so on, appointed not only to get things done but to keep us all safe.

This unconscious contract has its effects on the leader as well, especially when the projections of desire and dependency are not understood but believed. The result is that the leader develops an unrealistic sense of his or her own potency. This projection of need to be safe may be married with the seduction of power, and this creates the dynamic of co-dependency. In church life it is usually compounded by our language about God, which triggers all our regressive tendencies, for we are taught that God will keep us safe for ever.

Psychoanalytic theories of organizations explore this unconscious contract of transference and introjection that are an inevitable part of hierarchical organizations. Grounded in the seminal work done by Wilfred Bion[7] and Eric Miller and Kenneth Rice,[8] one of the most famous early papers was by Isabel Menzies Lyth,[9] who showed how the nursing function in a London teaching hospital operated as a defence system against the anxieties aroused in nurses by being so close to death and illness. Bruce Reed[10] and Wesley Carr[11] both worked at using these ideas to come to an understanding of some of the dynamics that operated in church life.

Put simply, we could think of the Church as a very safe organization into which we might project our feelings of anxiety. The theology of a loving father-like God, the liturgies and rituals which change very little, the role of the parish priest who provides high-quality pastoral care, all combine to provide a heady mix of unconscious transactions. In such a context we can regress and become child-like in our devotion to God and in our unrealistic belief and hope that all will be well. We expect our clergy to live under the public gaze; we dress them in a strange uniform; we put them on a pedestal and hope that they exemplify something we could never attain, and we punish them severely when they slip from that pedestal and behave like mere human beings. And from bishops we expect far too much and blame them when they do not fulfil all our expectations, false as they are. Monarchy in England and the Church are woven together in a fabric of co-dependency shaped in the early days of the Reformation. I am working on this chapter on the day in which a British prince and a woman called Catherine Middleton are married. The assumptions of the well-crafted sermon at the wedding and the cheering of the crowds as this young couple drive in an open carriage to his grandmother's palace reveal the potential in our culture – and maybe in every culture – for fantasy and make-believe.

However, the people we select to be our clergy and bishops often turn out to be exactly the kind of people who are keen to take our projections and begin to believe in them, so cementing this dependency culture into a fortress in which the price of safety for everyone is imprisonment and where, for clergy, the vocation to ministry is more often than not a calling to burn-out.

Two books by Larry Hirschhorn[12] mark an important change in corporate life. Much of the early work on psychoanalytic understandings of organizational life saw the organization as a steady reliable container for projection and transference. The organization was a defence against anxiety, and an essential capacity of its leaders was distance, steadiness and the ability to withstand all pressures by being well-defended. But in a rapidly changing environment, organizations have become much less stable and prone either to fail or to need radical and regular re-invention.[13] Hirschhorn argues that leaders in the post-modern organizational environment need to inspire confidence through their ability to show their vulnerability, as well as their entrepreneurial spirit. The spirit of the monarch needs to give way to the spirit of the 'wounded healer'. In such a world the transferences and projections change and need to be understood and responded to in different ways.

From quite a different perspective comes the work of William Kraus.[14] Kraus argues that all hierarchies believe in the value of competition and make it an essential feature of all organizational life. A rather circular argument goes like this. All people are inherently competitive, so to get the best out of them we need to create work environments that are competitive, and of course in their competitive environments workers behave just as it has been assumed they will. In hierarchies the structure looks like a pyramid so that you have to compete to climb the management ladder. Such competition for senior posts is alive and well in the Church of England. It always has been, but with more open processes for advertising and interviewing it becomes more obvious.

Kraus argues that this is a radical misunderstanding of inherent human nature. He sees humankind as basically collaborative rather than competitive, where sharing power and decision-making are most congruent with human preferences. Such a value system in the workplace, he says, among other things fosters inter-dependence, a high degree of individual control over immediate work environment, ongoing feedback, evaluation and modification, and problem-solving strategies rather than arbitrary resolution or political methodologies.

Some of the most contemporary writing about organizational life, and about motivation, points to this dislike of hierarchy being the future. Daniel Pink[15] has shown that autonomy, mastery and purpose are much more important than financial rewards. There are two exceptions to this. First, money is an incentive for those who do not have enough money to live on so that it is a constant worry to them. Second, when the tasks are very repetitive and require little brainwork, money does operate as an incentive. Other writers,[16] looking at some of the emergent new companies such as Gore and Google, have reported that new structures for organizing work are seeking to find patterns that eschew hierarchy.

This same trend has been apparent in some of the emergent churches, which have sought to find alternative patterns within hierarchy,[17] although they do not explicitly struggle with issues of leadership.

Before we move on we need to engage with the teaching of Jesus recorded in the Gospels about the kingly rule of God that he desired to bring into embodied living and into the experience of people. Many of his parables are about the kingdom of God, and it has been easy for the Church to associate the monarchy of God with traditional models of human monarchy and hierarchy. However, in one of the most explicit passages in the Gospels (Matt. 20.20–28; Mark 10.35–45; Luke 22.24–30) Jesus indicates that his understanding of the monarchy of God is exactly the opposite of traditional views of hierarchy, in that the God who is king, coming in the lived embodiment of Jesus, is a servant.

One cannot justify hierarchy from the teaching or the life of Jesus.

So, in summary, although in the world of business and in the Church there may be voices calling for an end to hierarchy, they are very few in number and in most places hierarchy is alive and well. Any church leader in such an environment needs to have his or her emotional antennae alert for those dark and dangerous unconscious forces that are the inevitable bedfellows of this paradigm.[18]

4

The warrior

Thou wast their Rock, their fortress and their might,
Thou, Lord, their captain in the well-fought fight,
In deepest darkness thou their one true light,
Alleluia.

O may thy servants, faithful, true and bold,
Fight as the saints who nobly fought of old,
And win with them the victors' crown of gold:
Alleluia.   (H.H. How, 1823–97)

From my birth I was taken to church by my parents, and I
spent many a happy hour in an old-fashioned Sunday School
which not only taught the stories about Jesus and his parables
but also the heroic stories of the Hebrew Scriptures. Joshua
who brought down the walls of Jericho; Gideon who overwhelmed the Midianites with so few; David who slew Goliath
and fled for his life from the fury of Saul; Shadrach, Meshach
and Abednego in the fiery furnace; and of course Daniel in
the lions' den – all took their place in my mind along with the
English archer heroes of Agincourt and leaders such as Wellington
and Nelson. In teenage years the stories of missionaries in India
and Africa, of William Carey, Hudson Taylor, Livingstone and
Moffatt were added to the list. Their clarity of vision, determin-
ation of purpose and willingness to suffer for the cause were
endlessly inspiring.

This heroic warrior paradigm leads to a particular reading
of Scripture. For instance, Jesus finds himself in a religious
culture which should be liberating but which is stifled by
regulation and political compromise. He sets himself against
the establishment and seeks to overturn it with his capacity

both to heal people and to teach them about his understanding of the God of Abraham, Isaac and Jacob. He becomes a revolutionary figure, fighting against all that he sees as evil. He rides into Jerusalem on a donkey, mobilizing the imagery of the key messianic picture from Zechariah and rivalling the entry of the Roman cohorts from the east. He associates himself with apocalyptic traditions, prevalent in the time of Roman occupation (Mark 13, etc.), that foretold the great conflicts and wars at the end of time.

This revolutionary conflict is re-enacted time after time in the stories of the Acts of the Apostles, first with the Jewish authorities, then between the Jewish and the Gentile Christians, then with the elders in cities in Antioch and Philippi, and finally with the Roman authorities. Paul takes such a conflict into the spiritual sphere with his language about principalities and powers and his use of military language.

> Put on the whole armour of God, so that you may be able to stand against the wiles of the devil. For our struggle is not against enemies of blood and flesh, but against the rulers, against the authorities, against the cosmic powers of this present darkness, against the spiritual forces of evil in the heavenly places. Therefore take up the whole armour of God, so that you may be able to withstand on that evil day, and having done everything, to stand firm. Stand therefore, and fasten the belt of truth around your waist, and put on the breastplate of righteousness. As shoes for your feet put on whatever will make you ready to proclaim the gospel of peace. With all of these, take the shield of faith, with which you will be able to quench all the flaming arrows of the evil one. Take the helmet of salvation, and the sword of the Spirit, which is the word of God. (Eph. 6.11–17)

Bill Hybel's books *Courageous Leadership*[1] and *Axioms*[2] make a fascinating read and they contain a great amount of wisdom. In the opening of *Courageous Leadership* he talks about a visit to Ground Zero soon after the attack on the twin towers in New York on September 11, 2001. He describes how he was impressed by the devastation, and by the heroism of the fire-fighters. He finds himself saying over and over again: 'No way.' The evil of the attack and the heroism of the workers provides the bedrock on which he builds his mantra that the local church is the hope for the world. These two things, a sense of the enemy and a single solution, inform the mind of the warrior. It is a very effective recipe for instigating action and it is not at all surprising that, for the warrior and for Bill Hybels, the key to leadership is the crafting vision and the 'casting' of it so that it inspires and motivates followers. Often one hears of any major project being described as a mountain to be climbed or a war to be fought, whether it be the building of a new auditorium or the eradication of poverty or HIV & AIDs in the Global South.

Many of the early British writers on leadership, such as John Adair and Wilfred Bion, forged their thinking about leadership in the Second World War. They developed ideas about officer selection, and the language of strategic objectives, missions, leadership development and battle plans seemed to transfer easily enough into the post-war world of reconstruction. Competition on the battlefield is not much different from competition in the marketplace.

Exceptional deeds are done by warrior leaders, and there can be no doubt that sacrificial deeds are done by those who follow them. Great stories are told by those whose sense of comradeship has been forged in the heat of warfare. But such a spirit has not only informed war. Many great changes in social welfare and charitable work are also fuelled by this sense of energy, vision and sacrifice. Where an enemy can be constructed and named, whether it is slavery, child poverty, capitalism or socialism, Christianity or Islam, then the energies of the warrior leader are released; the cause can be cheered and the battle can be joined.

It is not surprising that many of the warrior leaders in church settings have not only been charismatic people in themselves, but have also adopted charismatic styles of Christianity. The certainty of a direct line to God, the prospect of the end of time and the great judgement are natural metaphors to bind followers together and prepare them for the battles of faith to come. The 'great awakenings' in American religious life have been sustained and nourished by this warrior spirit coupled with evangelical and often Pentecostal flavouring.

Billy Sunday, a former baseball player, preached in the course of his lifetime to more than a hundred million people and is reputed to have said in prayer: 'Lord save us from off-handed, flabby-cheeked, brittle-boned, weak-kneed, thin-skinned, pliable, plastic, spineless, effeminate, sissified, three carat Christianity.'[3] The great preaching rallies of Jonathan Edwards, William Seymour, Aimee Semple McPherson or D.L. Moody with Sankey's songs, replicated later by tele-evangelists, were all effective within this warrior metaphor, sustained as it was by a growing belief that America with its huge resources and emphasis on freedom could win the world for democracy, capitalism and Christ.

Simon Western[4] devotes three of his chapters to exploring what he calls the Messiah discourse in leadership literature, and the close associations between the corporate world of the messiah leader and that of religious fundamentalism in the USA. He sees these similarities as being: over-identification with the leader, a drift towards totalistic vision and solutions, high rewards for followers and no place for dissent, and a stress on the culture of the organization.

While there certainly have been liberal warrior leaders[5] the majority have been attracted to a more evangelical and charismatic style of theology, devotion and music. There seem to be some essentials to a warrior leader, and the first of them is certainty. In the battle zone there can be no discussion about what is right or wrong: there has to be clear direction. For instance, it would be difficult to be passionate about converting Muslims if there were many aspects of Islam that command respect. Or if you are to join the battle against some evil that is identified, whether it be homosexuality, abortion, women bishops or naïve fundamentalist Christian faith, then it is necessary that you have no worries or doubts about the justice of the cause. There is something very energizing about this kind of certainty but it also brings to mind the work of Melanie Klein[6] and her insight into what has been called 'splitting'.

Klein, working out of a Freudian perspective, studied and treated children. She developed the theory that in very early childhood it is possible to identify three distinct phases. The first is dependency, in which the baby is wholly dependent on the primary carer for food and love, and in which all is well as far as the baby is concerned. But before long the baby realizes in the experience of loss and frustration that food does not come just when it is wanted, that all is not always well. The only way the baby seems to be able to handle this experience that carers are both good and bad is to see them as completely different beings, or 'objects', as Melanie Klein called them. In effect the baby constructs in its mind two different people, the good carer and the bad carer, and keeps them separate, so that it can love and be loved by the good and hate and be hated by the bad. Klein named these two 'objects' as the good breast and the bad breast and called this process splitting. She noticed that with splitting there is a release of a great amount of energy. Later on, as the baby grows, it realizes that the good and the bad are woven together in the same person and finds this puzzling and demanding a much more sophisticated response. It is impossible to love and hate the same 'object' at the same time. Klein noticed that the energy of the splitting phase gave way to a more depressed emotional state. It is much harder work to live with the good and the bad side by side, and Klein called this the depressive position. The implication of this kind of thinking is that the more you grow up into mature adulthood, the more able you are to hold things together, to see things from many angles, and the less likely you are to be seduced by the siren calls of what is evil and must be destroyed.

It also enables you to see that there may be several solutions to any problem that faces you. So much of our thinking seems to be restricted to an 'either–or' mindset which sees only two polar options for solving problems. Life is richer than that and much more complex.

Those of us who work within Kleinian ideas suggest that when we get under pressure the temptation is to regress, to go back into a former state of mind, which is easier for us and less demanding. So we slide downhill, as it were, from our grasp on reality into a black-and-white world in which it is easier all of a sudden to know what to do and to feel the energy returning. In such a frame of mind we seek for leadership that reassures us and keeps us safe. We are ready to march under the banner of a true and tested simple faith. The pressure on the leader to perform is immense, and the cost to both the leader and those who follow is that they have to collude to agree to live in a world that denies its complexity.

Churches that live within this paradigm place great store on the unity of the congregation and the sense of being all together, and dissenters soon realize that their perspective is not welcomed. I remember as a teenager reading the book *Who Moved the Stone?* I was asked why I could not just accept it all and give up asking questions. It was a strange response when the book was all about proving the resurrection, but it alerted me to the pressure to conform and to be an obedient disciple rather than a questioning one.

While it is essential that all leaders are trustworthy, it seems much more important for the warrior leader to be a role model for his or her followers. These leaders' own lives of bravery, risk and sacrifice become the stories that are told and the biographies that are written.

Thinking back to my own introduction to English history, it was more or less a history of wars, battles won and valiant leaders. I learned nothing about social class, poverty, the growth of democracy, agriculture, industry or the impact of culture, or how men and women have lived in social relations through the ages. Rather, it was Harold, Richard the Lionheart, Henry V at Agincourt, Robert Bruce at Bannockburn, Drake and the Armada, Nelson at various sea battles, Wellington at Waterloo, and so on. Warriors are heroes and it is no bad thing in itself that followers do their best to emulate their heroes – much more healthy than today's worship of celebrities where it seems the desire is not to be like them but to have what they have.

However, the combination of the charismatic leader and a large band of devoted followers with a simple mantra and a great marching tune can be dangerous. The paths of the warriors are lined with the broken reputations of some of the most famous. A study by Roland Howard of the Nine o'Clock Service[7] in Sheffield and its leader Chris Brain makes interesting and very sad reading. In his introduction Howard writes:

> Underneath the carefully manicured exterior, the real story is of a man who seemed, according to many, to have a megalomaniac desire to control other people: of a complex, secretive organization, where unknown to many, abuse existed; of a leadership convinced that their leader was God's mouthpiece who was going to save Western civilization.

But it is not an isolated story. See, for instance, the exposure of Ted Haggard, who campaigned against homosexuality but also had a long-term relationship with a gay prostitute. In his resignation he said, 'There's a part of my life that is so repulsive and dark that I have been warring against it all of my adult life.'[8] I quote this to draw attention to the military language.

I have started with these two paradigms of the monarch and the warrior because they are by far the most common in all church life. The monarch provides safety and stability and organizational effectiveness, while the warrior provides growth and huge achievement. They both have substantial biblical support and a long history in the traditions of the Church. However, I believe that they carry within them risky and sometimes deeply disabling dynamic processes that militate against the mature growth and development of both leader and follower, because they rely for their strength on the capacities of regressive and infantilizing projections. In a monarchy, the people may be safe but they do not mature because they are not allowed to find their own voice or struggle for themselves with the realities of life. In the warrior paradigm, they may achieve great things and have great energy but in the end they sacrifice complexity and reality and dwell in a dualistic world of good and evil.

Both monarch and warrior resort in the end, and sometimes from the beginning, to the use of force. As Adam Kahane says: 'Either people involved in the problem can't agree on what the solution is, or the people with power – authority, money, guns – impose their solution on everyone else.'[9] This has never been the way of Jesus, and it provides all of us who are appointed to positions of leadership in the Church with the most complex and spiritually demanding vocation.

There is another way of constructing a narrative about the divide between these two paradigms and the others that follow. Gordon Lawrence[10] introduces the idea of consultants working out of two differing political stances. The first he calls 'salvation' and the second 'revelation', both of which are well-known terms in theological discourse. The first, coming from a modernist view, holds the belief that things can be managed. An organization has a problem and calls in a consultant with the expectation that the expert from outside will be able to fix it and save the organization. From a psychoanalytic perspective Lawrence calls this the 'rescue phantasy', and Richard Sennett has a wonderful illustration of just this, quoting the research done by Georgina Brown in her study of the result of John Birt's use of McKinsey consultants to restructure the BBC. He writes:

The consultants, mostly young men with recent MBA degrees, learned about the business in the process of re-engineering it . . . The McKinsey consultants took little responsibility, however, for implementing these changes, nor did they deal with the human consequences of changes; among these consequences were large numbers of people shifted from areas in which they had developed expertise to areas in which they were driving blind . . . The consultants were paid, and then departed leaving the organisation in turmoil.[11]

Christianity, with Jesus as a saviour, falls into this frame of thought so easily, and the monarch and the warrior both see themselves as some kind of a saving leader.

The politics of revelation, on the other hand, lead to a style of consultancy that is collaborative and where the process of discerning what really is wrong and discovering what might emerge as an answer is worked at together by both the consultant and people fully involved in the organization. From a Christian perspective we might think of revelation as that which comes from right outside, transcendentally, but there is an equally valid way of thinking of revelation as emerging from within, through the dwelling of the Holy Spirit. It is this spirit of revelation, rather than a spirit of salvation, that infuses the following paradigms.

5

The servant

Brother, Sister, let me serve you,
Let me be as Christ to you;
Pray that I may have the grace to
Let you be my servant too.   (Richard Gillard)

It has generally been my experience that the very top people
of truly great organizations are servant-leaders. They are
the most humble, the most reverent, the most open, the
most teachable, the most respectful, the most caring, and
the most determined.   (Stephen Covey)[1]

I was in Canada in 1985 on a visit with some other British
Christian adult educators, funded by the Fellowship of the
Maple Leaf, when I came across two things which I count as
milestones in my own thinking. The first was to discover that
there were Christians who found it very difficult to refer to
God or Jesus as 'Lord'. It was a word I used without thinking,
almost as an adjective: the Lord God or the Lord Jesus Christ.
Yet here were some people whose Christian discipleship and
ministry shone brighter than mine who found the word 'Lord'
unhelpful and in some cases repulsive. For them, I discovered,
the word resonated with the days of imperial power, monarchy
which was British and the House of Lords. All these things
they had cast away as their country had become independent
in 1867 within the Commonwealth. Their reading of the Gospels
and their faith had no place for monarchy, lordship or the language of dominance. I began to learn again about the potency
of the language we use and the ways it shapes our assumptions
about so many things – gender, race, class and, of course, religion
and God.

And it was on that same visit that I first sang the words which head this chapter. It was a moving experience for me and still is, even though it is now a popular hymn in most of our contemporary hymnbooks.

It was only later that I was introduced to the ground-breaking work of Robert Greenleaf.[2]

Robert Greenleaf was born in Terre Haute, Indiana, and spent most of his organizational life in the field of management, research, development and education. He was also a member of the Society of Friends.

When Greenleaf retired in 1964, he coined the term 'servant leadership', and wrote and spoke extensively on the subject. In 1970 he published 'The servant as leader', an essay which launched the servant leadership movement in the United States.

In his essay he refers to the short novel by Hermann Hesse, *The Journey to the East.*[3] The story recounts a journey made by a community of pilgrims in search of the ultimate truth. They journey with a servant named Leo, who is described as happy, pleasant, handsome and beloved by everyone, and who has a rapport with animals. However, he disappears at a particularly hard part of the journey. Leo cannot be found and is soon blamed for stealing objects thought at the time to be of crucial importance but which, when they eventually turn up, are found to be of no importance at all. Finally the community disintegrates and the pilgrimage is abandoned. The pilgrim who tells the story later finds out that Leo was not merely a servant but also a key leader of the community, and his leaving was some kind of test that they all failed.

This movement for servant leadership is based on a fundamental belief, which is that humankind only survives and functions in community. Perhaps taking up the idea in Genesis that it was not good for Adam to be on his own, this point of view affirms that our capacity to serve is essential to our make-up. I shall unpack further the meaning of the word 'serve', but it would not be going too far to say that we are all born to be servants: that is, born with an innate tendency to work out how we can behave for the benefit of the others with whom we live.

We had an interesting discussion with the Bishop's staff of the diocese of Oxford when we introduced these servant leadership ideas as the core of our programme. We wondered whether Jesus was born a leader who chose to be a servant from among many choices of leadership style, or whether he was born a servant who could only lead as a servant.

There are many biblical references to servanthood. The servant songs in Isaiah stand out, as do the sayings of Jesus about his coming among us as one who does not lord it over us but serves.

Each of Isaiah's songs emphasizes key elements of being a servant and forms the foundation for all subsequent thinking among Christians about the meaning of being a servant.

> Here is my servant, whom I uphold,
> my chosen, in whom my soul delights;
> I have put my spirit upon him;
> he will bring forth justice to the nations.
> He will not cry or lift up his voice,
> or make it heard in the street;
> a bruised reed he will not break,
> and a dimly burning wick he will not quench;
> he will faithfully bring forth justice.
> He will not grow faint or be crushed
> until he has established justice in the earth;
> and the coastlands wait for his teaching. (Isa. 42.1–4)

> Listen to me, O coastlands,
> pay attention, you peoples from far away!
> The LORD called me before I was born,
> while I was in my mother's womb he named me.
> He made my mouth like a sharp sword,
> in the shadow of his hand he hid me;

he made me a polished arrow,
in his quiver he hid me away.
And he said to me, 'You are my servant,
Israel, in whom I will be glorified.'
But I said, 'I have laboured in vain,
I have spent my strength for nothing and vanity;
yet surely my cause is with the LORD,
and my reward with my God.'
And now the LORD says,
who formed me in the womb to be his servant,
to bring Jacob back to him,
and that Israel might be gathered to him,
for I am honoured in the sight of the LORD,
and my God has become my strength –
he says, 'It is too light a thing that you should be my servant
to raise up the tribes of Jacob
and to restore the survivors of Israel;
I will give you as a light to the nations,
that my salvation may reach to the end of the earth.'

(Isa. 49.1–6)

The Lord GOD has given me
the tongue of a teacher,
that I may know how to sustain
the weary with a word.
Morning by morning he wakens – wakens my ear
to listen as those who are taught.
The Lord GOD has opened my ear,
and I was not rebellious,
I did not turn backwards.
I gave my back to those who struck me,
and my cheeks to those who pulled out the beard;
I did not hide my face
from insult and spitting.
The Lord GOD helps me;
therefore I have not been disgraced;
therefore I have set my face like flint,
and I know that I shall not be put to shame;

he who vindicates me is near.
Who will contend with me?
Let us stand up together.
Who are my adversaries?
Let them confront me.
It is the Lord GOD who helps me;
who will declare me guilty?
All of them will wear out like a garment;
the moth will eat them up.   (Isa. 50.4–9)

For you shall not go out in haste,
and you shall not go in flight;
for the LORD will go before you,
and the God of Israel will be your rearguard.
See, my servant shall prosper;
he shall be exalted and lifted up,
and shall be very high.
Just as there were many who were astonished at him
– so marred was his appearance, beyond human semblance,
and his form beyond that of mortals –
so he shall startle many nations;
kings shall shut their mouths because of him;
for that which had not been told them they shall see,
and that which they had not heard they shall
    contemplate.
Who has believed what we have heard?
And to whom has the arm of the LORD been revealed?
For he grew up before him like a young plant,
and like a root out of dry ground;
he had no form or majesty that we should look at him,
nothing in his appearance that we should desire him.
He was despised and rejected by others;
a man of suffering and acquainted with infirmity;
and as one from whom others hide their faces
he was despised, and we held him of no account.
Surely he has borne our infirmities
and carried our diseases;
yet we accounted him stricken,

struck down by God, and afflicted.
But he was wounded for our transgressions,
crushed for our iniquities;
upon him was the punishment that made us whole,
and by his bruises we are healed.
All we like sheep have gone astray;
we have all turned to our own way,
and the LORD has laid on him
the iniquity of us all.
He was oppressed, and he was afflicted,
yet he did not open his mouth;
like a lamb that is led to the slaughter,
and like a sheep that before its shearers is silent,
so he did not open his mouth.
By a perversion of justice he was taken away.
Who could have imagined his future?
For he was cut off from the land of the living,
stricken for the transgression of my people.
They made his grave with the wicked
and his tomb with the rich,
although he had done no violence,
and there was no deceit in his mouth.
Yet it was the will of the LORD to crush him with pain.
When you make his life an offering for sin,
he shall see his offspring, and shall prolong his days;
through him the will of the LORD shall prosper.
Out of his anguish he shall see light;
he shall find satisfaction through his knowledge.
The righteous one, my servant, shall make many righteous,
and he shall bear their iniquities.
Therefore I will allot him a portion with the great,
and he shall divide the spoil with the strong;
because he poured out himself to death,
and was numbered with the transgressors;
yet he bore the sin of many,
and made intercession for the transgressors.

(Isa. 52.12—53.12)

51

I first met Bishop Njongonkulu Ndungane when, as the new Bishop of Kimberley and Kuruman, he formed a partnership with Bishop Richard and the diocese of Oxford. On his retirement as Archbishop of Cape Town, Sarah Rowland Jones edited a series of essays in his memory.[4] Allan Boesak writes one of the essays, with the title 'Servant leadership in public life'. He admits that the idea of servanthood has been completely devalued in South Africa. However, he reminds readers of the constant emphasis by Bishop Njongonkulu on servanthood:

> 'How,' he asks, 'dare we speak of servant-hood today?' Only, he answers, if we ourselves become servants of the One who made himself a servant for us, Jesus of Nazareth. He willingly gave away his power, which he was free to hold onto. He washes feet. He makes room for others. He redefines servant-hood by challenging and overturning the paradigm of domination and power, and doing precisely what he was not required to do but does it anyway, out of love. Jesus does not ask others to be his servants. He invites them to be his friends, and then he serves them, feeds them with his own body and blood, his life. And this is how Jesus relates to people, not as a ruler, but as a friend and servant.

It is easy to think that there is an apparent contradiction between being a leader and a servant, and if you ask a group of people to make a list of appropriate adjectives to describe a servant and another list for a leader, there will be few adjectives that fit in both columns. Yet at the heart of the Gospels is the man Jesus, who had no difficulty with the assertive leadership of vision and at the same time washed his disciples' feet.

In his essay Greenleaf put forward what he called the best test of a servant leader. He asks:

> Do those being served grow as persons; do they while being served, become healthier, wiser, freer, more autonomous, more likely themselves to become servants? And what is the effect on

the least privileged in society; will they benefit, or at least, not be further deprived?

In the handout used in our training material, Mike Williams, one of our tutors, summarized the characteristics of servant leadership:

> The primary characteristic of a servant leader is the recognition that the problems encountered are not 'out there' but 'in here'. So fundamentally a servant leader begins with the realisation that such leadership is a journey of self-discovery and they have the desire to change as a result of what they learn about themselves.

1 Listening receptively: Many who lead only listen to themselves or a few close allies. The servant has to know what are the real needs of those being served. To give undivided attention through listening receptively is hard work but fundamental to being a true servant.

2 Acceptance of others and having empathy for them: This is about striving to understand and put oneself in the shoes of the other. It is based on the acceptance and recognition of the gifts and good intentions of others who are fellow human beings.

3 Exert a healing influence: Learning how to help heal difficult personal and organisational situations aids the development of wholeness and trust.

4 Highly developed powers of persuasion: Reliance on persuasion rather than authority or coercion is fundamental to maintaining the self-respect of others.

5 Awareness, foresight and perception: General awareness both of oneself and emerging patterns helps develop an integrated approach to problems and to anticipate ethical issues. Lessons from the past and the reality of the present help to discern the course of decisions for the future.

6 An ability to conceptualise and communicate concepts: To point the way servant leaders need to be able to dream great dreams, listen to the prophets and give people a sense of vision. It is the ability to look over the horizon and tell people what you see.

7 Commitment to the growth of people: This is based on the belief that people have an intrinsic value beyond their ability to fulfil some role or job. Servant leaders are committed to the personal, professional and spiritual development of people.

8 Practising the art of contemplative reflection: Stopping and taking time to review and reflect before making key decisions. Keeping in touch with the spiritual dimension of life and putting situations in context.

9 Building community: Servant leaders seek to build a sense of community based on trust and dialogue among those being served.

10 Stewardship: A recognition that we are stewards and hold things in trust for the greater good of society and future generations.[5]

Another perspective comes from Robert Dale:

> Servanthood as a leader stance encouraged by biblical materials has several practical implications.
>
> Servants lead out of relationships, not by coercion. Servants don't demand obedience or submission. They meet their followers at the point of need. Servants have a common touch, maintain living contacts, and demonstrate consistent concern for their followers.
>
> Servants lead by support, not by control. Servants give from themselves rather than take for themselves. They love and lift others rather than manipulating them.
>
> Servants lead by developing others, not by doing all the ministry themselves. Servants, whether clergy or laity, recognize that the kingdom of God calls for the full participation of all believers. All spiritual gifts are given by God for service to Christ's body (Eph. 4.11–13).
>
> Servants guide people, not drive them. Volunteer organizations like churches require selfless leaders rather than selfish bosses or bullies.
>
> Servants lead from love, not domination. Authority, in part, grows out of 'the consent of the governed'. Peter sounded this theme clearly: 'Tend the flock of God that is your charge, not

by constraint but willingly, not for shameful gain but eagerly, not as domineering over those in your charge but being examples to the flock' (1 Peter 5.2–3).

Servants seek growth, not position. Servants aren't ambitious. They keep the growth and spiritual health of others paramount. Unlike Diotrephes, an ambitious leader in the early church who preferred to 'put himself first' (3 John 9), servants put others first.

Servanthood is obviously a demanding, high-risk leadership stance. But faith is demanding and risky too. Servanthood is full of crosses as well as towels and basins.[6]

From a practical standpoint we found ourselves in Oxford coming to some tentative conclusions about two hallmarks of a servant leader. First, in a church setting, if you are a servant leader you will always be growing other leaders around you, and you will have real joy in seeing others take up leadership and even more joy when these new leaders do better and go further than you could yourself. There will be no envy and no clinging to position power.

Second, as a servant you will always be seeking to work in collaborative and team settings. This will not only be a strategy to foster the growth of leaders but will be because you know that you do not have all of the answers. You will know that together, and in company with others, you will find greater wisdom, spiritual insight and strategic clarity.

So there are two questions. Are you growing people around you into leadership? Are you always working in collaborative and team settings? Peter Senge[7] asks: 'How many people perceive you *first* and *foremost* as a servant?' What does it take to cultivate a genuine desire to serve? He goes on to say 'Genuine servant leadership is deeply personal and inherently collective.'

There is something that needs to be made very clear. A monarch may choose to operate in ways that have servant qualities, and most hierarchs in churches claim to do their best to act as servants, but at the end of the day, when all attempts at persuasion have failed, monarchs can and always do resort to their position power and use their power to force the outcome they require. For example, there is a person in your church who is on the rota to read the lessons on Sunday. But this person does not prepare, mumbles and cannot be heard, yet refuses to use the amplification system even when it is switched on and everybody else uses it. You have held some training evenings to help all the readers do better. You have given feedback and it has made no difference. You have tried every way you can think of to influence and persuade this person. You know that every time he or she gets to read the lesson the worship is spoilt, not only because the lesson cannot be heard but also because this individual is representing some stubborn and unspiritual force. You discuss this with your trusted elected officers or other colleague ministers and come to a shared point of view that this behaviour is unhelpful.

If you work wholly within a servant paradigm there is nothing you can do, except keeping on serving the person concerned. But as a monarch, at the end of the day you have the power to remove him or her from the rota. You will then, in your role as minister or 'priest in charge', be in control and for all the best reasons will use the power that your position has given you. You will have, to use another phrase, forced your will, even if it is the collective will of some democratic process. The person removed from the rota will know that in the power dynamics of the church you have the power and he or she does not.

From an organizational perspective this power may be needed, and at Sarum there are occasions when persuasion is not enough and behaviour, especially behaviour that can bring danger to others, needs to be challenged and stopped. But I am left with two overriding problems. The first is that I cannot find anywhere in the Gospels any instance when Jesus used position power to force his will. He was undoubtedly outspoken and forceful in his speech, but in the temptations he explicitly rejected the prospect of using his power to bring about his wishes, he never sacked his disciples, and on the cross he chose the way of service rather than power. Of course, it was not long after the day of Pentecost that the new community of faith began to put in organizational structures and with these came positions of power. Indeed, many of the texts that we have in our Christian Scriptures provide evidence of the Church struggling with how much power Christians should have over one another.

The second is more personal. It has to do with my experience of how God deals with me and how God's love for me works, and this shapes how I think about love. I cannot find any experience in my life in which it has seemed as if God was forcing me into a deeper relationship. Of course, God longs in love to create and reform and renew and transform me closer to my created potential, but the love that I experience from God is always an invitation that can be rejected rather than an order that has to be obeyed. Indeed, it seems to me that obedience is the destruction of love, and those people who use love as a reason for abuse and forced obedience are among the most to be feared. This then becomes for me a deep truth about life and the ways of God, that love cannot force its desires or will and can only, in the rejection of those approaches of love, suffer. This for me is the majesty and mystery of the experience of Jesus in the garden, when he chose the way of suffering after an intense discussion with God and when, despite all the world could throw at him, he chose to stay loving. For me the cross is the final act in a life of love and also its crowning glory.

There are two settings where servanthood has most chance of real expression. The family has in almost all cultures been the way of organizing intimate small communities. Over the centuries and in different cultures the family takes different patterns and forms but, whether arranged or self-chosen, two people agree to live together and may bring new persons to life and maturity among them. Most parents discover that as children grow it is less and less appropriate to try to use force to win agreement. Many are the struggles with teenage members of a family when force becomes worse than useless and often counterproductive. Families can be places of absolute hierarchy with either patriarchal or matriarchal power. It is also true that violence in the family is deeply rooted in British contemporary culture. It may well be that without organization power and structure, and with the failure of loving to be as strong and creative as it can be, then violence grows out of desperation. But in a loving family one can find the closest example of the love of God freely given and freely received.

Church should also be an attempt at creating community life in which love is the fundamental principle. I often wonder what it would be like if the Church could be a kind of foretaste of what God really wanted for us all. In the search for new expressions of church, many seek non-hierarchical styles of leadership and are seeking to learn from the monastic traditions. There is a longing that church should be the kind of community in which love alone shapes the ways we listen to one another, speak our minds knowing we will be heard, and find solutions which build self-esteem and maturity. Such communities are places where the young are honoured and the poor are given pride of place.

There are, however, criticisms of servant leadership which need to be taken seriously.

The first comes from some women whose lives have been shaped by the overriding sense from our cultural heritage that women should be servants. Household chores, part-time low-paid work and child-rearing have been thought of as low-value roles. These people feel that the modern emphasis on servant leadership has the unhappy consequence of undermining the proper leadership of women and entrapping them once again in a culture of subservience and domesticity. It is important to note the contextual significance of these resonances, but it also alerts us to a more general criticism that servant leadership allows the powerful to always get their way and the leader to be at the beck and call of any who announce themselves as being in need. It can be said that the culture of service does many clergy a real disservice in that it becomes a way of life that enables them to collude with their failure to be themselves, or to learn to say 'no' in a way that is reasoned and loving, and to continue to work long hours to the detriment of all. The servanthood of Jesus was strong, not weak; it was assertive and not pathetic; it was a doorway rather than a doormat. It is interesting to note in passing that some women find this paradigm less upsetting and fully engage with it as an alternative to the monarchy that they see in so much church life, and which as women they have disliked.

A second criticism says that servant leadership based on the life of Jesus is theologically inadequate. Jack Niewold[8] argues that servant leadership thrives on a Christology that emphasizes a Christianized humanism and has been separated from some of the orthodox doctrines of a more complete understanding of Christ, who is not only the suffering servant on the cross but also the king of history. I find this to be a weak understanding of servant leadership, set out in order to link it with modern liberal humanism before discarding it. It cannot be said that Jesus was enacting servanthood while on earth but that as Christ he is 'lord' of all he surveys. The Jesus on earth has to fully embody the godhead for any view of incarnation to be viable, and so the God of all time has to be understood in terms of the kingdom teaching and living and dying of Jesus. My understanding of 'kingdom' is that the kingly rule of God is the rule of love, and the power of God is the potency of love, and that while it is in the nature of God to be loving it cannot be in the nature of God to be 'in charge'.

The final criticism of servant leadership comes in a much more telling argument based on the words of Jesus reported in John 15.15, in which Jesus says: 'I do not call you servants any longer ... but I have called you friends.' A theological understanding of friendship has a long taproot. Indeed, discussions about friendship go back a long time. Aelred of Rievaulx wrote extensively about friendship, and two more recent studies are those of Michael Vasey[9] and Liz Carmichael.[10] Stephen Pickard,[11] after a masterful survey of writings on collaborative ministry, notes that friendship has not been a theme in writings about ministry. He goes on to suggest that friendship is often discouraged among ministers and their congregations, and this is certainly what I experienced in my training. He argues that friendship should describe a mode of togetherness that might lie at the heart of collaborative ministry.

Perhaps friendship and servanthood are companion categories for ministry and leadership. As such they belong together. They are not simply different options that present themselves for appropriation. Nor are they simply complementary forms of ministry. Rather they inhere each other; they too are 'one of another'. Together friendship and servanthood make collaborative ministry what it is and inform the manner in which it is undertaken. This means that collaborative ministry is for ever a fragile and suffering ministry that lives by trust and joy. It is the way in which Christian disciples learn how much indeed they are 'one of another', faithfully following the pioneer ministry of Jesus Christ.

6

The elder

Wisdom cries out in the street;
In the squares she raises her voice. (Prov. 1.20)

The elders meet at the entrance of the village. They will generally be older men, no longer much use for heavy work in the fields. They will tell the stories of the past and remind themselves of their origins. They will no doubt be wondering about the behaviour of the young people in the village and bemoaning the changes that have occurred during their lives. They will be there to settle disputes between neighbours. More often in the past they would have been men, but in some cultures they will have been the communities of wise women to whom people turned for comfort, healing and wisdom. There is no election, nor birth priority, but a gradual discernment among the community that this person has the wisdom to belong to the eldership. Rather like the ancient tradition of spiritual direction, you find out that you are one when you are sought out and asked to be one.

Michael Sadgrove, in his wonderful book on wisdom and ministry,[1] argues that much of the wisdom literature in the Hebrew Scriptures emerged from the royal courts where young people were trained in the art of being wise as a requirement for their future public leadership. He quotes Plato from *The Republic*: 'Until philosophers are kings ... and wisdom and political leadership meet in the same man [*sic*] cities will never cease from their evils – no, nor the human race.'[2] He goes on to draw out aspects of wisdom from the history narratives as well as from the Psalms and the classical wisdom literature. The capacity to handle complexity, to understand the way the world works and the ways that people respond, to go deeper and get to the meaning of things, to have a moral compass and integrity and to be fearless, and above all to know one's place in relation to God, are all aspects that he draws out with an elegance of writing that is both simple and profound at the same time. It may well be that the origins of wisdom literature are in the courts, but I want to suggest that this wisdom tradition lies deeper in the hearts of tribal communities. Vincent Donovan in his book *Christianity Rediscovered*[3] draws this out in the way he discerns the elder in the village who is already priestly.

The key aspect of this wisdom tradition is that it invites you into a discussion and leaves you to ponder and respond and make up your own mind about an issue. In the end the monarch will issue an order and the warrior will exhort you to belong and join the comrades in the struggle, but the elder will invite you to a conversation in which, in the end, you have to decide. This is exactly the way of Jesus in so much of his teaching ministry. He tells a parable and says: the only thing for you now that you have heard my story is for you to make your own sense of it. 'Let anyone with ears listen!' (Matt. 11.15; 13.9). Jesus goes on in this last passage to spell it out more clearly: 'The reason I speak to them in parables is that "seeing they do not perceive, and hearing they do not listen, nor do they understand"' (Matt. 13.13). We only have one occasion when we are offered an interpretation of a parable in the Gospels and that is the Sower. Jesus does not explain it to the crowds but is reported as explaining it to the close inner circle of disciples. But even this explanation is full of ambiguities and we are still left puzzling over whether we are the seed which is expected to multiply or the ground into which it falls and germinates. For generations we have argued over the sayings of Jesus about wealth and divorce and pacifism and we are still working out what belongs to God and what belongs to Caesar.

Theodore Zeldin gave a series of talks on BBC Radio 4, which were later published,[4] in which he extols the importance of conversation as a way to change the way we think and perhaps to change the world. He stresses that in a conversation we need to be open to the ideas and thoughts of the other person and prepared to change our mind. This is quite different from an argument, in which we do our best to persuade the other person to our point of view, knowing full well that we are decided and will never change our minds. The history of the Church is littered with debates which have turned into heresy trials and schisms simply because we have never learned to live with difference and allow the kind of conversation that Zeldin describes. Far too much of our religious experience is shaped by fear, and fear becomes an essential tool of totalitarian regimes, whether they be national or religious. We are fearful that we will not be accepted and will be excluded. We are fearful of being isolated from the community that gives us a sense of esteem and identity. We are fearful of eternal punishment. So we close our minds and learn obedience. We deaden the very creativity of God that is seeking to shape us to be human.

Every time you are faced with something that puzzles you and you discuss it with friends and in the end come to your own decision, you are exercising your freedom and your responsibility. You are more fully inhabiting the world that God has given us in which to work out what it means to be made in God's image. Every time you do what you are told without thinking, you opt out of the calling that the early stories in Genesis seem to indicate God has imagined for us all.

At Sarum College we have worked hard at developing our understanding of what wisdom means, and at a recent Sarum Conference on the theme of wisdom our Director of Studies was able to introduce the conference with these words that we have crafted together:

At Sarum College, our philosophy of education is summarized by our mission statement: we are an ecumenical centre for Christian study and research where our passion is learning that nourishes the human spirit. Ecumenism for us means bringing together, in mutually respectful conversation, scholars and practitioners from across the Christian Churches . . . Our mission is fulfilled when our students come away from their time at Sarum College spiritually nourished and academically equipped. Our students witness to this spiritual nourishment through lives marked by wisdom and courage. For us, developing wisdom in our students means being able to foster in them the skills of a generous interpreter; one who can hold in tension a variety of viewpoints and perspectives. It means helping students become the kinds of people who explore issues with intellectual and emotional knowledge; who can live with the language of poetry and metaphor as well as science and reason; who are able to allow the stranger or the alien to challenge any tentative conclusions; and who can stay both provisional and at the same time decided. While becoming wise means that our students become conversant in such principles and skills, becoming courageous means that they are emboldened to translate such principles into transformative action. Our students are encouraged to apply their wisdom in the world, whether in vocational ministry, professional careers, social work, education, or political life.[5]

There is an endless struggle between the desire to live with the complexity of life and a regressive longing to make things simple and easy. This is not the way of the wisdom tradition, where there are no simple answers and where we never stop learning and need to stay open to the thoughts and feelings of others (Prov. 1.8). This is the way in which truth learned long ago is reformed and reshaped in the light of experience and new contexts (Prov. 15.2, 7; Eccles. 12.9).

I want to illustrate this with reference to a way of working in leadership programmes that has become almost universal and is known as action learning. The origins of action learning are attributed to Reginald Revans.[6] In essence an action learning group (often known as a set) is a small peer group that meets to help each other learn by using a disciplined framework. The time is divided equally between the members, who each in turn present an issue that they are facing in their lives about which they are still undecided or unresolved or for which they cannot find a solution that satisfies them. The peers in the group listen and think about this puzzle or problem and respond by asking the presenter questions, and the more open the questions they can ask the better it is.

The rule of asking questions requires one to really listen. Warren Bennis says about his early work with T Groups at Bethel:

> The most important thing I learned was to listen, to truly listen . . . Listening is an art, a demanding one that requires you to damp down your own ego and make yourself fully available to someone else. If you listen closely enough, you will hear what the speaker means, whatever the words. And paying undivided, respectful attention inevitably makes you more empathetic, one of the most important and undervalued leadership skills.[7]

Through his work with groups, Bennis came to believe that democracy was inevitable, and even predicted that the Socialist Soviet empire would dissolve. They were post-war days of optimism with an unquestioned belief in enlightenment and capitalism. But when we think about metaphors that might speak to contemporary culture in the West it may well be that the elder metaphor has a great deal to bring to the table.

This rule of asking questions has several real and significant benefits. It starts with the conviction that the person with the problem is best placed to understand the complexities of the context and to engage his or her own capability to respond. This individual is uniquely placed and is the only one who can come to a conclusion about how and where and when to act. Of course, in a team setting the person may do that with others. Questioners need to stay attentive and not be diverted by their own desire to solve other people's problems. It helps everybody to develop the skills of questioning so that away from the group the same skill can be applied. It undermines any desire to be competitive and fosters a strong spirit in the group of service and equality.

Here, for example, are some of the questions we have found over the years to be useful. Set out here they may seem rather abrupt; the way in which they are asked is often as important as the question itself.

What options have you considered?

What do you think you might not be noticing?

If you had a blind spot in this situation what might it be?

How long have you been worrying about this?

How long before you act?

When this happened, what did you feel? Can you name that feeling?

How long might it be before you try something else?

How did the other protagonists feel, or how did you think they felt?

If you could trade in those words for another set of words, what other language would you like to trade it for, e.g. 'judged' – 'affirmed'?

What difference does it make being a Christian in this situation?

If you can't change the situation by an action, how can you change it by the way you think about it?

Can you discern any pattern in your life? Have you had this dilemma before, and if you have, has it happened often? What did you do before?

What would need to happen for you to feel differently about this problem?

What is there about this situation that excites you, frightens you, depresses you?

When you pray about it, is there anything God says to you?

If you were to take a God's eye view of the situation, what
would it look like?

What would Jesus do?

Are there any riches from the Christian tradition that throw
light on this situation?

Where is the gift in this situation?

Where is the darkness/sin?

What are the best and worst possible outcomes?

What don't you know about this situation and how could
you find it out?

What's holding you back from acting?

This spirit of enquiry seems to me to be close to the heart of God.
Alongside other streams of narrative there is definitely one that
shows us God not laying down the law but rather enquiring. In
the garden of Eden God says, 'Where are you?' This first question allows the man and the woman the freedom to stay hidden,
but they choose to come out from hiding (Gen. 3.9). Soon after,
God finds Cain and asks him where his brother Abel is. Cain does
not answer but parries the question with one of his own.

This same spirit of enquiry is found frequently in the way
Jesus related to people. At the key moment of disclosure at
Caesarea Philippi, Jesus asks the question about what others
are saying about him and more directly to Peter: 'But who do
you say that I am?' (Matt. 16.15). On the way to Jericho, either
James and John or their mother comes and asks Jesus for pref-
erential treatment and Jesus responds with one of the most
telling questions of all time: 'Are you able to drink the cup
that I drink, or be baptized with the baptism that I am baptized
with?' (Mark 10.38). In Jericho, when Blind Bartimaeus is
brought to Jesus he makes no assumption that he knows what
this blind man wants and asks him: 'What do you want me to
do for you?' (Mark 10.51).

Stephen Cottrell, in the introduction to his short book on
the Easter stories, writes:

It is therefore striking and significant that many of the things Jesus says are questions: 'Why are you weeping?' 'Who are you looking for?' 'What are you discussing?' 'Was it not necessary . . . ?' Taken that the other common thread running through the resurrection stories is the fact that Jesus isn't recognized, these searching questions have the effect of confronting us with a risen Christ who cannot be easily pinned down ('Do not cling to me' he says to Mary), who demands response. It is not a coercive demand. It is more the magnetic attraction of great and puzzling beauty; the sort of beauty that takes us beyond ourselves. Just as great art poses great questions, so does the resurrection of Christ.[8]

The first book of Peter chapter 5 is important in that Peter identifies himself as a fellow elder. Whether this comes from Peter's hand or from a follower of his using his name to give added weight to his thoughts does not undermine the fact that he is seeing himself or is seen within the community as sharing eldership.

It is the Society of Friends which most obviously echoes the influences of the elder paradigm. They have no ministers, but elected elders and a clerk to the meeting whose responsibility is to test the mind of the meeting with tentative conclusions to see if they command assent. A fundamental aspect of their life together is their worship, in which people sit in the round and ministry is offered as the Spirit moves. Each ministry is received in prayerful silence and there is usually a significant time of silence after each ministry so that the ideas and thoughts can be held in the mind and heart. Each ministry is held in respect as the listeners seek to hear the prompting of the Spirit of God both in the person and in what has been said.

Even more significant is their basic text alongside the Bible, which is called *Advices and Queries*.[9] In each section there are basic tenets of faith and practice and a series of questions known as Queries. Often a ministry in the meeting for worship will use one of these Advices and Queries, and what is significant from my point of view in this chapter is the use of an open question. Here is their first section.

1 Take heed, dear Friends, to the promptings of love and truth in your hearts. Trust them as the leadings of God whose Light shows us our darkness and brings us to new life.

2 Bring the whole of your life under the ordering of the spirit of Christ. *Are you open to the healing power of God's love?* Cherish that of God within you, so that this love may grow in you and guide you. Let your worship and your daily life enrich each other. Treasure your experience of God, however it comes to you. Remember that Christianity is not a notion but a way.

3 *Do you try to set aside times of quiet for openness to the Holy Spirit?* All of us need to find a way into silence which allows us to deepen our awareness of the divine and to find the inward source of our strength. Seek to know an inward stillness, even amid the activities of daily life. *Do you encourage in yourself and in others a habit of dependence on God's guidance for each day?* Hold yourself and others in the Light, knowing that all are cherished by God.

4 The Religious Society of Friends is rooted in Christianity and has always found inspiration in the life and teachings of Jesus. *How do you interpret your faith in the light of this heritage? How does Jesus speak to you today? Are you following Jesus' example of love in action? Are you learning from his life the reality and cost of obedience to God? How does his relationship with God challenge and inspire you?*

5 Take time to learn about other people's experiences of the Light. Remember the importance of the Bible, the writings of Friends and all writings which reveal the ways of God. *As you learn from others, can you in turn give freely from what you have gained?* While respecting the experiences and opinions of others, do not be afraid to say what you have found and what you value. Appreciate that doubt and questioning can also lead to spiritual growth and to a greater awareness of the Light that is in us all.

6 *Do you work gladly with other religious groups in the pursuit of common goals?* While remaining faithful to Quaker insights, try

to enter imaginatively into the life and witness of other communities of faith, creating together the bonds of friendship.

7 Be aware of the spirit of God at work in the ordinary activities and experience of your daily life. Spiritual learning continues throughout life, and often in unexpected ways. There is inspiration to be found all around us, in the natural world, in the sciences and arts, in our work and friendships, in our sorrows as well as in our joys. *Are you open to new light, from whatever source it may come? Do you approach new ideas with discernment?*

I have highlighted the Queries in italics.

If you seek to live within this paradigm you will find the courage to speak your mind in the company of your peers with the trust that it will be weighed and valued and built upon even if not accepted. You will welcome those who may not agree with you but whom you know you can trust. You will be passionate and vulnerable; you will have opinions but know they can be changed.

7

The contemplative

O living flame of love that wounds my soul so softly in its deepest centre.[1]   (St John of the Cross)

I have got this far in the book without mentioning the word 'holy'. It is the contemplative paradigm that brings the idea of holiness into the foreground of any thinking about leadership. Henri Nouwen's little book[2] on leadership provides a fine starting place.

Nouwen had a career in which he became a well-published and famous speaker as well as an academic theologian at Harvard. He gave all that up and went to work in a L'Arche community in which one-to-one care is given to people with profound disabilities. Nouwen tells the story of his caring for Bill Van Buren and the journey they took together to a conference in Washington, and how throughout his speech and after it Bill took some initiatives which could have been deeply embarrassing but which demonstrated in word and action the very ideas that Nouwen was talking about.

In three short chapters Nouwen turns much of the contemporary thinking about leadership on its head. Each chapter has three sections: the temptation, the question and the discipline. The first chapter has as its title 'From relevance to prayer'. The temptation is to be relevant, the question is 'Do you love me?' and the discipline is that of contemplative prayer.

Nouwen sees the first temptation of Jesus, to turn stones into bread, as a temptation to be relevant and competent. This is matched in today's world by the desire to be successful, highly regarded and relevant. However, this desire seems to shield us from the deep anxiety about whether we are loved. 'I am telling you this because I am deeply convinced that the Christian leader of the future is called to be completely irrelevant and to stand in this world with nothing to offer but his or her own vulnerable self. This is the way Jesus came to reveal God's love'.[3] Nouwen goes on to remind us that the risen Jesus did not ask Peter whether he would grow the Church or bring people to faith or be successful, but rather whether he loved him.

A short passage on the discipline of contemplative prayer is worth quoting as it says it with an elegant and vibrant beauty.

> Through contemplative prayer we can keep ourselves from being pulled from one urgent issue to another and from becoming strangers to our own and God's heart. Contemplative prayer keeps us home, rooted and safe, even when we are on the road, moving from place to place, and often surrounded by the sounds of violence and war. Contemplative prayer deepens in us the knowledge that we are already free, and that we have already found a place to dwell, and that we already belong to God, even though everything and everyone else keeps suggesting the opposite.   (pp. 28–9)

It is easy, in a world that looks for outputs and results and in a church which seems to reward those who over-work and are endlessly busy, to lose this absolute priority for prayer, meditation and contemplation.

Nouwen sees the second temptation, in which Jesus is asked to throw himself from the temple, as echoing our modern desire to be spectacular and popular. The third temptation reveals our longing for power. The desire for popularity is redeemed by vulnerability and by collaborative ministry in which there are no heroic solo efforts. The call this time of the risen Christ is 'Feed my sheep'. The longing for power is held in check by the last words of Jesus in John's Gospel, telling Peter that he will be taken and led where he does not want to go. Here is the familiar but impossible demanding call to sacrifice and obedience to the will of God.

While it is true that there is often a close association between a mystic and a contemplative, this is for me a different focus. John of the Cross, who wrote some of the greatest mystical poetry, was also a reformer, working for a radical change of monastic life, and the mystical experience came out of his effort and suffering as much as his contemplative discipline. However, they are linked in their capacity both in deep contemplation and in the experience of union with Christ to enter more deeply into the sufferings of Christ and of the world.

As I have tested out some of the ideas that I am writing about, I have been urged to have a paradigm of God-bearer, based on the experience of Mary the mother of Jesus. I have resisted because it has seemed too gender-specific for me. The Scriptures give us a picture of Mary as the contemplative person, keeping so many things in her heart. And it is no surprise that many of the mystics have been women, for whom the intimacy of the love of God has seemed natural. One only has to think of Hildegard of Bingen, Beatrice of Nazareth, Mechthild of Magdeburg, Hadewijch of Antwerp, Marguerite Porete, Margery Kempe, Thérèse of Lisieux, Teresa of Avila, Julian of Norwich and more recently Evelyn Underhill, Ruth Burrows, Maria Boulding and Simone Weil, to name but a few.

For the contemplative, holding God in your heart and knowing that you are precious in the sight of God and loved for who you are forms the foundation of any attitude or action. I remember working for a short time alongside a priest who always seemed to be more interested in worship than mission. It was a parish with a daily Eucharist, and morning and evening prayer were the required practice of the ministry team. In discussion he would say that he was not called to be successful but faithful. He had confidence in God in such a way that the work of mission and bringing in the kingdom belonged to God and not to him. At one level he drove his parishioners crazy because the activists among them wanted more than just prayer, but at another level he followed in the long stream of those who always put prayer at the centre of any discernment, whether that came from an evangelical or a Catholic expression of church.

It is interesting that the most popular study days for clergy in the diocese of Salisbury at the time of writing are those entitled 'Contemplative ministry'. It could be possible, of course, to see this as a retreat from engagement in the demanding tasks of leading the Church. One could go on to suggest that this flight to contemplation is a failure of nerve in the midst of so much marginalization of the Church and its apparent failure to 'make its mark'. It would be possible to see it as a last desperate grasp at some miraculous cure for themselves and their parishes. But I think it is a desire to connect more fully with this paradigm and to claim something absolutely distinctive for Christian leadership.

8

The prophet

Every celebration of the mass is a political act.

(Dan Berrigan)

When there are prophets among you,
I the LORD make myself known to them in visions;
I speak to them in dreams. (Num. 12.6)

The ecumenical movement was alive and well when I was at Bristol University in the late 1960s. It was a time of ferment and student occupations. Each denomination had its own society but we joined in an Association of Christian Societies. There was a radical Christian magazine called *Roadrunner* and I think it was in there that I first read about Daniel Berrigan.

I was going through some significant personal reappraisals. I had been brought up an evangelical Baptist on the south coast of England. I knew nothing of the history of dissent and the place of the Baptist heritage in non-conformist history. I knew nothing of the persecution of dissenters in the seventeenth century. Non-conformists who voted substantially for the Liberal cause until they discovered Lloyd George's infidelity deserted political involvement and opted instead for a kind of personal piety. That was certainly the flavour of the lively church of my youth. Going to the Baptist theological college in Bristol introduced me to the history of dissent and it seemed to fit me much better than the piety of my teenage years.

Dan Berrigan[1] was a Jesuit American priest who was active in the protests against the Vietnam War, and became famous for breaking into US military offices, celebrating the mass and then burning the draft papers with napalm. He went underground and was hunted by the police, and finally caught and imprisoned. What has stayed with me is the quotation from him with which this chapter starts.

To my knowledge there is only one book on leadership which is about dissent, and it is written by Gerald Arbuckle.[2] He argues that all organizations should foster dissent among their ranks. He argues that the healthy future of any organization is to be found not only in the leadership of the hierarchy but also in the leadership that emerges in dissatisfaction and dissent, and in the conflicts between them. It is worth remembering that every new movement in church life has come from dissatisfaction with the status quo, and often battles with it. This is true whether it be the development of every monastic movement, the Reformation, the charismatic movement, the Oxford Movement, Methodism or the more recent 'emerging church' phenomenon, to mention just a few. Arbuckle is writing for a Catholic audience in the years after the Second Vatican Council and is calling on religious congregations 'to embrace their true vocation to prayerful asceticism and prophetic action which are at the very heart of religious life'.[3]

The Hebrew prophets are held in honour for their consistent critique of their contemporary life, of religious practice as well as social justice. They sought to bring the light of God and shine it on whatever evil was revealed. Sometimes this was done by telling a story, as when Nathan went to David (2 Sam. 7) or when Jesus told parables against the scribes and Pharisees (Mark 12). On other occasions it was effected by somewhat bizarre attention-seeking actions which are often overtly political, for example when Jeremiah puts a yoke on his neck (Jer. 27), or when Jesus rides into Jerusalem on a donkey, matching the Roman cohorts' entry from the other side of the city, and disturbs the economics of the temple (Mark 11).

What is distinctive about prophet leadership is that it completely undermines the rather popular idea that you know you are a leader because when you look over your shoulder you notice people following you. Prophet leaders may well look over their shoulder and find that all their followers have deserted them (Mark 14.50). More than that, prophets will often find themselves arrested, put in prison and ostracized. It happened to Jeremiah, Jesus, Mohammed and many others.

In my experience prophecy expresses itself in two different ways. The first kind of prophet is deeply involved in some kind of ministry, almost always among the poor and needy. Out of that perspective, the prophet finds a voice that cries for justice, an end to evil abuse of power and a redistribution of wealth. This voice is heard in the public square and always has a political edge. It is the voice of Amos, Jeremiah, Nathan (2 Sam. 12), John the Baptist or Helder Camara, assassinated at the altar of his cathedral while celebrating the mass. Such a prophet priest is a friend of mine, Robert, in an urban priority area of great deprivation where he has been the vicar for twenty years.

Much of what follows is in Robert's own words, which he has given me permission to use, but first I want to reflect about what is revealed to be a fundamental clash of cultures that Robert's words bring to light. The great tradition of the Anglo-Catholic missions to the inner cities was about living in the midst and ministering there, whether or not people came to church. Success was never measured by numbers. However, these days many in the Church, and especially our bishops, are mesmerized by numerical growth in the same way that our politicians are addicted to economic growth.

There is a spirituality that lies at the heart of the prophet that grows out of and feeds into an incarnational presence. After a tough time in his own life, Robert writes about the spiritual tradition that revived him:

> Do not give up, then, but work away at it till you have this long-ing. When you first begin, you find only darkness, and as it were a cloud of unknowing. You don't know what this means except that in your will you feel a simple steadfast intention reaching out towards God. Do what you will, this darkness and this cloud

remain between you and God, and stop you both from seeing him in the clear light of rational understanding, and from experiencing his loving sweetness in your affection. Reconcile yourself to wait in this darkness as long as is necessary, but still go on longing after him whom you love. For if you are to feel him or to see him in this life, it must always be in this cloud, in this darkness. And if you will work hard at what I tell you, I believe that through God's mercy you will achieve this very thing, 'strike on that cloud of unknowing with a longing dart of love' (from *The Cloud of Unknowing*[4]).

Something had happened. Shifted? Deepened? I thought no more about it until, using the formal prayers of the Church, I found myself aware, in a very new way, of who it was that I was addressing: Almighty and Eternal God, and Father . . . If I were to use other metaphors, I was addressing Kindly Darkest Pit, Eternal Embrace waiting for me within Depth of Void. I came, in prayer, to rest in silence, in this awareness of any one of my dark, hard, hurt places. I came to see movement out as taking a risk, approaching the edge, to rest again in the darkness and the hurt. I was led to take up ministry in a place, often described as an 'open prison', the dark holy place of the riots of 1981, the home of a criminalized community. It is also the same community in which, in 1943, I was born, the first time.

This tradition of spirituality seeks no return in success or promotion, and offers a spiritual togetherness with the most disadvantaged and damaged people of our world, that they know and recognize. Writing to his bishop, he says: 'I am also the Vicar to them of the Parish. I am not a Judge, nor the Police, nor a Manager – I am a Priest, I Am for Them; I wait on their deep ambiguities.'

Robert writes about his ministry and offers an example from a funeral.

In a short time, I came to understand what I had never appreciated before: How a 'secular', a 'multi-cultural', multi-Faith-&-none, deeply ambiguous and contradictory Community, the 'Parish', could regard the 'Parish Church' as THEIR Church. In their own way, they 'used' it, 'worked with' it. They were not 'poor' people needing the Church. They were 'mature' people using the Church to deal with those things they could not deal with anywhere else ... They could deal with [other] things elsewhere ... The Parish Church was one of those places where they dealt with the things they cannot deal with!

... Church-warden stood up front, in front of the coffin and under a huge Crucifix suspended then from the roof, before offering the 'Kiss Of Peace':

'Now I know that you on my left (the Women and Friends of the Deceased) blame you on my right (Friends of the Sons of the Deceased and 'drugs cartel' for whom the Sons are the 'God-fathers' and in Prison and on Remand) for the death of Mrs S. (She was killed by the joy-rider of a stolen car, a high-powered red Ford-Escort, 'high' on the drugs bought from the 'cartel'). And I know you on my right (The 'cartels' all in their black specs, and the partners and sons and brothers of the women on the left) are furious at the Police and Warders for not bringing the S Brothers here today, as promised ...

Well, for today, for her behind and him up there [pointing], I want you to say to me 'And Also With You' when I wish you the Peace. Then I want you to cross that divide in the middle and go wish Peace ... GO ON!! [They all did, stutteringly at first, then with laughter and slaps on the backs.]

As I led the Coffin and Bearers down the aisle at the end of the Service, glad that I had survived and I was getting out, a 'Big Black Guy' in dark specs leaned out to me. I thought I was to be 'head-butted', he said, instead, 'That was a fuckin' marvellous service, vicar.'

... The STORY continues: Chief Inspector of Police talking to Deanery Clergy weeks later recalled the 'event' and told us the Women had later gathered in their Men to the Club, next door to the Synagogue, and told them to lay off the pushing of hard-drugs (crack-cocaine was appearing in the Community at the time) and the stealing of high-powered red Ford Escorts (a Granby–Toxteth speciality) – And that if they didn't, their Women would reveal to the rest of the Community the 'hidden skeletons' of their Men. The Chief-Inspector reported a complete drop in those particular crime figures.

Robert writes about the threatened closure of the only church-aided school in the area, and writes in one of his regular 'epistles':

> Our School, is to close, primarily for small numbers. During Advent, every Wednesday for 3 hours, I am holding a Vigil of Grief: A 'soft' Protest at the loss of a 'Good' School to a hard-pressed Community . . . and the likes of Muslim Children gaining access to 'main-stream culture' – outside the Town Hall, by kind courtesy of the Vicar of that Parish. I have two banners with the slogans 'YOU KNOW SMALL NUMBERS WORK' and 'DEAR H.M. GOVERNMENT(S), CITY COUNCIL, DIOCESE, YOU KNOW SMALL NUMBERS WORK. SIGNED, MULTI RACE, MULTI FAITH, MULTI LINGUAL, ST M's School'. Twos and threes gather, and comment that small numbers do work in ways that large numbers can not.

There was a long letter of complaint to the bishop about lack of consultation with him or with his PCC. He also drew attention to the perspective of the police, who had talked about the lack of trouble from children from the school, about the school as 'a leaven for good' within the community. On another occasion he writes:

> *I do believe*, where possible, or how possible, and as I have said a few times in Deanery Chapters passed, the 'Management' of the Church for England can keep confidence in the 'parochial system' where there is still a Priest and still a Community Parish, to offer 'patronage', boundaries and support, for working with 'being lost' and the Church's vulnerability – I must offer a Prayer Workshop on 'The Transcendence of Vulnerability In Situ', and maybe call it 'Good Grief!?'

As prophets are always close to the edge, it is not surprising to read: 'In our fight for our School, I heard from another Governor, that a contact of his in the House of Lords, from another Lord, from his Nephew, that Robert Gallagher is regarded in the Diocese as a trouble-maker running a shrine of six people.'

I have here presented one side of the picture and I am sure there would be many reasonable counter-arguments, but I want to help us all get into the mind and spirit of a prophet. The Church of England has over the centuries developed a careful balance of power between episcope and parish priests holding the freehold. While many a bishop may have thought the words of Henry about Beckett – 'Who will rid me of this turbulent priest?' – on the whole there has always been a place for prophet priests. However, clergy have said to me that they sense that this tolerance, indeed welcome, of the prophet is coming to an end. Economic pressures on the Church have led to an uneasy marriage between organizational strategies at diocesan level and a desire for bishops to be more managerial. Deaneries are expected to develop mission and deployment plans and increasingly the prophet priest does not fit in with such neat and tidy strategies. Measurable outcomes in terms of numbers of people attending church and financial stability and self-sufficiency seem to outweigh the outcomes of holiness, pastoral care and concern for social justice.

However bizarre the language and actions, however disconcerting the ideas, however troublesome to the hierarchy, such prophet leaders are essential to the health and renewal of the Church.

There is a second expression of prophecy which has become more familiar with the recovery of charismatic experience. This gift of prophecy is often associated with visions and dreams. In the Western world we are familiar with the work of psychoanalysis and its emphasis on dreams. The ideology of the Enlightenment focused on the person as an individual, so when Freud began to make sense of patients' dreams he thought they belonged to and referred to their personal life. Those of us brought up on Bible stories knew that the dreams of Joseph, Pharaoh, the Butler and the Baker (Genesis 37—41) and Daniel were seen to have political and social implications. This idea of corporate or social dreaming has been recovered by Gordon Lawrence.[5] Freud knew that dreams were strange phenomena which knew no boundaries of time or space, and in which symbols were chaotic but significant. What we have recovered is that dreams are not only – or perhaps not at all – about how I got on with my mother, but more about our social and political relations. In tribal communities a dream will be brought to the elders of the village or to the shaman for shared interpretation. In the Church, following the instructions of Paul, dreams and visions are brought to the community for interpretation and affirmation.

I woke one morning recently having dreamt that I had been running along a cycle track beside a busy road. As I looked down at my feet I noticed that they were more like the splayed feet of a dog than my own. I realized that I felt as if I was a wolf loping along on a long chase after prey, and noticed that it felt as if I could go on and on without losing energy. I remember wondering if I would be less exhausted if I had wheels, but saw a pram and thought those wheels would be too bumpy for the long haul.

I wondered what this dream might mean. Could it be about me and an unconscious concern that I was getting older and maybe could not keep going? Could it be about a client I had seen the day before who had been exploring what was significant given that he was ten months into a new parish post? Might it be about our college, which is embarking on a fund-raising project? Whose dream was it? Was it mine, about me? Had I been given the dream that really belonged to the priest I had seen but who might not have remembered it or made use of it? Was it a dream for the college? Was it a dream that had been given by God? All these may seem bizarre questions but, in the realm of the spirit, visions and dreams are experiences where the boundary between the earth and heaven is permeable.[6]

The prophet leaders, from whatever background or spirituality, share the same purpose, which is to bring to light and make known the ways and wisdom of God, either as a light to show the way or as a searchlight to expose what longs to remain hidden. I have been thinking about this chapter during the weeks when both phone-tapping by journalists and the systematic abuse of vulnerable adults in care homes have been exposed. I have been thanking God for the prophets and whistleblowers among us.

9

Taking the strain

The waves have some mercy, at least, but the rocks have no
mercy at all.   (Irish proverb)

Each sword-opened side is the matrix for God
To come to me again through travail for joy.
                        (Eugene Peterson, 'The pain')

Whether you are tea trolley workers on a broken-down train
or the most powerful chief executive in the world, or a team
member chancing your arm to make a suggestion about a better
way of doing something, there is always the risk of losing your
humanity. Sometimes it is the dynamics from your unconscious
or your own unrecognized neediness that leads you to believe
the fantasies you are developing about yourself. Sometimes
it is simply the adoration of others and the hopes they invest
in you. Sometimes it is the unrecognized patterns of desire or
fears in your own life that surface from time to time.

Eugene Peterson writes about the seduction of market forces
and commercial ideas that are so prevalent in the American
churches.

> I do not find the emaciated, exhausted spirituality of institu-
> tional careerism adequate. I do not find the veneered, cosmetic
> spirituality of personal charisma adequate. I require something
> Biblically spiritual – rooted and cultivated in creation and
> covenant, leisurely in Christ, soaked in the Spirit.[1]

In 1996 Marlene Cohen, herself the separated wife of a senior
Christian leader, wrote a small book called *The Divided Self*[2]
in which she explored some of the dynamics of leadership from
the perspective of those narratives of clergy who behaved

in ways, usually sexual or violent, that have destroyed their ministry. While the Roman Catholic Church has been in the spotlight for such failures in recent years, every bishop, superintendent or district chair knows of those people under their own care who have crossed boundaries of proper conduct, and the secrecy they have engineered. Indeed, recent editions of *Leadership Today* have focused on pastors in the USA who have acknowledged addictions to pornography. So often such leaders have impressive public lives but murky private fantasies and, often, violent family lives. The gap between faith and behaviour seems to open up a fissure of human failure. Others have explored these more extensive failures in depth[3] and the vast majority of ministers and Christian leaders keep well clear of trespassing over these boundaries. However, in my work with clergy I have found that stress, depression and poor or ineffective leadership often come when people cannot hold together what they believe, how they feel and what they find themselves doing.

Similar issues seem to arise in many who choose a career in the helping professions. Robin Skynner[4] develops theories about a pattern of behaviour where caring professionals, without realizing it, end up dealing with their own needs for care. They therefore misplace much of their care and the expression of their needs. The solution, Skynner insists, is self-awareness, along with rigorous supervision which explores the worker's personal needs as much as the way that worker is caring for the needs of his or her clients.

I have suggested that the risks are much greater for those who exercise leadership as monarchs or warriors and much less for those who exercise leadership as servants or in a team of elders, but the risks are real to all who take up leadership roles. In talking over some of my ideas with others, it has been suggested that each paradigm is attractive at some level to people as a defence against some shadow or dark aspect of their personal history and identity. It seems to me to be possible that the lure of hierarchy defends against the fear of desertion, the attraction of the warrior against rage, the elder against isolation and the taking of personal responsibility; the desire to be a servant may defend against unhealed wounds, and that to be a prophet against a sense of belonging and the loss of a sense of self; it may be that the contemplative fears the failure of attempted actions.

In this chapter I want to develop a way of understanding the pressures and suggest strategies for taking the strain in ways that enable to you stay healthy as a leader.

Marlene Cohen suggests it is easy for Christians to believe that their 'old nature' has been redeemed and no longer has power in their lives, but she identifies eight stages of self-knowledge:

- Awareness that I do dysfunction
- What actually happens when I do?
- When does it happen?
- Do I really want to change it?
- Why do I do these things?
- Who suffers when I do them?
- Where did it start and how did it grow in me as a pattern?
- Do I know how to change it?

In working as a mentor to leaders I have found the idea of role as a kind of second psychological skin to be helpful. The first skin is the one that you grow for yourself as you journey through life. It makes you the kind of person you are and is the result of the way you have responded to life as it has happened to you. Some of it will be genetic and biological and some of it will be environmental, and it seems pointless to speculate too much about which is which. Together, especially in early life, these will give you the kind of disposition you have, extrovert or introvert, happy or miserable, full or empty of self-esteem. This skin, like physical skin, can allow things through, so you can adjust your sense of self, adapt to circumstances, take new directions, become more or less open to experience. At the same time it is a skin, so some things can be bounced off. In school others can make concerted efforts to make you feel bad about yourself, and you either absorb these pressures, take them in and reshape your sense of self, or you can resist them. And so we grow our skin to be tough, pliable and vulnerable. Herein lies the endless interior negotiation that makes us human. For instance, in mid-life, say, some catastrophe happens and we lose through death someone who is close to us. If our skin is too tough we defend against the experience of pain and grief and bounce it away and cannot take in the experience, be changed by it and grow through it. If, on the other hand, our skin is not tough enough we can be overwhelmed and be unable to contain the experience and be transformed by it. In either extreme we become unwell, and the loss of a managed sense of self begins to feel like madness. Healthy people are those who can experience whatever life brings, weave it into the story they tell of themselves and at the same time enlarge their capacity to contain and understand their emotions. We often call this self-awareness, and it is an essential attribute of all leaders.

This self-awareness is a major plank of those who talk about emotional intelligence,[5] and it is important to stress here that awareness covers a range of perspectives. It probably does not need to be said, but when we are attending to other people we listen to the words they say, we listen to the way they say them, we notice things about their facial expressions and what we call their body language. And at the same time we need to listen to the way we hear and attend, both intellectually and emotionally. Goleman identifies these two skills of emotional intelligence as noticing what is happening to us as we listen, in both our thoughts and our emotions, and at the same time managing those emotions that we are noticing. It is worth noting that for several centuries in the West we have been dominated by an over-reliance on intellect. Indeed, when I was at theological college at the end of the 1960s it was the clearly stated belief of the principal that if he could teach us to think he could teach us to handle whatever came our way in ministry. He was the product of his generation and he possessed a fine academic mind, but I quickly learned that ministry was to make demands on my emotional life as well as on my intellect.

'Role' refers both to functions that we find ourselves choosing or having to take and also to our relationships. So I become a brother, son, lover, husband, father and learn the ways of being those roles or functioning within them. Some I chose, such as husband, and some I had no choice in, such as brother. Priest or minister would be another that I chose. Being in a leader role, whether in a formal position or an informal one, would be another one that I chose. I realize that it can feel as if some of these roles are thrust upon us. We talk about being called to ministry, or sometimes people force us to take up a role, but I want to stress that, whatever the force, in the end we take responsibility and say 'yes'. Some of these roles have a permanent feel to them; I have been a brother for all of my life so far and will probably remain one, unless my two brothers die before I do. Other roles may be much more temporary; I was priest in charge of the Upper Kennet Benefice for just two years, and the tea trolley workers in the broken-down train may only have had the informal role of being leaders for a couple of hours.

Most of the time when we look for a job, or as a minister look for a new church or parish, we study the offered role that is set out in a job description and hope for something that we think will be a good fit. Sometimes that works and sometimes we discover that the fit is much more complicated than we expected. We want to do the job in one way but colleagues or managers or parishioners want us to do it in other ways, and there develops conflict around the way the role is carried out.

Returning to the metaphor of skin, the best image I have found so far is that of a wet suit, dry suit or diver's suit. Sailors, surfers and divers use both wet suits and dry suits, depending on how cold the water is. Both fit the body pretty tightly and provide a thermal layer. In a wet suit, hands, feet and neck are exposed and the water creeps up inside the suit and then takes the temperature of the body, but you feel the wet and the cold! A dry suit is just as flexible as a wet suit but keeps the water out, so you stay dry. If you want to go deep enough and withstand high pressure then you will need a diver's suit. In a diver's suit you are completely enclosed and can move much more slowly, connected as you are to the ship on the surface which provides oxygen and a way of lifting you out of the water when you are ready.

The question for any leader has to do with how we relate to the environment in which we lead, and how we handle the pressure and emotional temperature. If you like, the choice a leader takes is how cold or wet we allow ourselves to be, how defended we appear in order to preserve our sense of self. People who have taken up the role of counsellor or psychoanalyst have a very great understanding of how role and person skins interact with one another and the ways in which unconscious processes can breach the boundaries. All leaders who seek to lead from a faith perspective, and especially leaders in church settings, are equally at risk, whatever paradigm we think we have chosen as the best fit for ourselves, and it is worth setting out why this might be.

People who come to church enter a culture that is distinctive for two specific reasons. First of all they embrace a language about God and humankind that encourages a kind of dependency that is very deep. We use Father language about God most of the time, we emphasize our human failures and sins, we kneel at an altar rail to be fed, we long for redemption and sing songs about how good and reliable God is to deal with all our problems, we call ourselves children (of God). This kind of regression is a powerful dynamic that can shape our relationship with figures of authority and leadership. At the same time church life and language sets a context that is eternal and includes life after death. In more evangelistic circles this can be used as a threat, and some of the great Victorian evangelists dangled listeners over the fires of hell to bring about a conversion. The potency of life after death is obvious in Islamic extremist suicide bombers. Whether it should be or not, the promise of heaven or hell is a motivator and, combined with the languages I have already referred to, deepens the unconscious desire for harmony, peace, salvation and a leader I can put on a pedestal.

So I suggest that the strain is very significant for all those in Christian leadership, and within the tradition there have always been ways of seeking to understand and respond creatively to such strain. The obvious response is to concentrate on one's spiritual life through prayer and daily study of Scripture, and for an Anglican priest this is expected to be a daily discipline. For some a regular retreat is also part of the strategy to reduce stress. But we have a remarkable capacity for self-deception, either that our own prayer life is good enough and can sustain us, or that we fall so far short that we feel we are running on empty most of the time. What seems to me to be essential is to find a critical friend.

The first kind of critical friend comes within a frame that has been known as spiritual direction, although these days it has the more appropriate name of spiritual accompaniment or soul friendship. You search out a person whom you know to be grounded in reading and understanding of the great spiritual traditions, and who has a wisdom that you can trust. Then in the intimacy of a confidential conversation you talk about and explore the ways in which your relationship with God is shaping your practice as a leader. These conversations will generally help you to remember that you are loved by God and do not need the affirmation of the congregation, nor do you need to be undermined by their criticism, even if you come to realize that it is justified. Your soul friend will help you to laugh at yourself; will help you to recall that the mission is God's and not yours, so bringing perspective to your efforts;

will help you call to mind your sins in a context in which you will know that they are forgiven; will extend your capacity for self-awareness.

By way of an example: soon after taking up my present post I was going to see my spiritual director and wanted to talk about how I was feeling empty inside. I found myself thinking of myself as a rather old gnarled tree that was hollowed out inside but still growing branches and leaves, rather like an old tree in the field near our house. In conversation we explored together whether it was more important to me to be hollowed out and apparently dead from the inside or to be growing and alive on the outer edges of the tree. That became a conversation about where I expected to find the presence of God in my life. On this occasion there was no discussion about what was on my mind in terms of my new role nor the challenges and opportunities that were facing me. We might, but did not on that occasion, have explored why I felt such a strong need to be a tree that had no defects, nor did we talk about my tendency to want to earn affirmation by my work rather than just to know myself loved as I am. Both those discussions have been on the table on other occasions, and in some sense can feel rather like therapy. Of course, in the relationships between two mature people the boundaries between therapy, spiritual accompaniment and consultancy are very flexible. I drove home from my conversation less anxious.

The second strategy is very similar in that it too is a conversation with a wise critical friend. It has a variety of names – coaching, mentoring, consultancy – and although there are technical differences these cover more or less the same ground. To be more precise, coaching assumes that the coach knows a lot about the skills you need to do your job and can teach you; mentoring has more of the feel of being with someone who understands the context and the issues because your mentor has been there and done the kind of job that you now have; consultancy comes somewhere between the two in that you might expect the consultant to have some understanding of the issues you face as well as some strategies and skills in helping you to understand or act in new ways. While spiritual accompanying focuses on your relationship with God, mentoring focuses on your exercise of ministry as you have been experiencing it. Many of the outcomes mentioned above will be similar, although there may be some clearer focus on ideas and strategies for leading and managing in the particular situations that you bring for discussion.

Here is another example: I was recently working with a senior manager who was in the last months of bringing about a merger of two organizations. He had already been appointed to a new job in the merged organization but was at the same time still on the board of one of the original concerns, working alongside a team of executives, all of whom were looking for new posts. The organization was performing excellently. I noticed that my client sounded and felt rather flat emotionally, and this led us to a conversation about the inevitable grieving process for the merging organizations and the need to contain the anxiety and sense of loss, as well as to lead the vision for the new merged organization.

Robert Young describes psychoanalysis in a way that fits very well with consultancy and spiritual accompanying:

> the issue is not one of content but of capacity, not what is contained but that there should be a suitable container so that we can do for ourselves and our loved ones what a good analyst does: take things in; hold, ruminate and detoxify them; and, if seemly, let them out again in good time and in good measure so that they can be of some constructive use in facilitating thought, feeling and constructively relating.
>
> . . . to find a way of treating mental space as available for containment, a place where one can bear experience, hold it and be able to ruminate it, metabolize it, reflect upon it, savour it. The meaningfulness of experience is always under threat. It may be batted away or used to locate, amplify and feed madness

and then be reprojected or reduced to cliché or collapsed into despair. The point of capaciousness is that it should serve as a container for thought, and the point of thought is to keep emotion alive. Without emotion there are no viable relationships, and without relationships there is no world.[6]

Both these strategies for support bring self-awareness and self-acceptance, are not enough on their own and need to be supplemented with a wide range of both theoretical and practical skills. There is a wonderful phrase: 'If the only tool you have is a hammer you will treat everything as a nail.' A good leader will do all he or she can to learn new skills and acquire new tools.

Taking the strain is also a matter of health. Some years ago at one of the Willow Creek Leadership Summits a sports coach called Jack Groppel[7] talked about the importance of recovery. He offered an interesting thought that there is no such thing as too much stress, there is just a matter of not enough recovery time. He illustrated this from his work with top-level athletes, who intentionally stress their bodies to the limit and do so without damage by managing excellent recovery. He talked about tennis players who recover between long and demanding rallies. I have found it to be an excellent way of thinking about work and life, and over-work and long hours, by simply asking where the recovery time is. It resonates with the ideas of Stephen Covey[8] in his *Seven Habits of Highly Effective People* in the section called 'Sharpen the saw'. Here he writes about the four essential ingredients for staying healthy: keeping the body fit, keeping social relationships and friendships nurtured, keeping the brain and intellect alive, and nourishing the spirit.

Talking about physical fitness can be a tricky subject these days, but it is brought into focus by the work of some women writers on leadership.[9] Amanda Sinclair has a chapter called 'Bringing bodies into leadership', and calls to our attention the whole issue of embodiment, the way we dress, the way we stand, the way we talk. She reminds us that it has been part of the patriarchal discourses on leadership to ignore the body because it draws attention to gender issues.

I vividly remember two related experiences during my first visit to Toronto. The first was attending my first Anglican Eucharist with a woman priest presiding, and the second was sitting quietly for an hour in a small garden at Emmanuel College in the presence of the sculpture by Almuth Lütkenhaus-Lackey called *Crucified Woman*. At the first, all the robes of Catholic tradition were there, along with acolytes and incense. What made the difference for me was the voice alone. At the second the naked body of a woman was suspended with arms outstretched, where normally we only see the body of a man.

Sinclair argues that while the body, with its shape, posture, voice and dress, is very important in all exercises of leadership there is little written about it, suggesting that it is part of a discourse that assumes something that is specifically gendered. She notes that many of the narratives of leadership show leaders able to work long hours without rest, doing their daily exercise (there seems to be nothing so good as showing the US president out for his daily workout) and having bodies that never wear out or tire. This mystique of command over the body is evidence that a person should have command over situations and other people.

This means that as a leader you need to pay attention to the impact your physical presence makes. How you stand, how fit you are, how tall or short you are, how over- or under-weight you may be, all have impact. Sinclair suggests that for women there is the issue of how they portray the feminine condition of 'pregnability', when so much of the leadership discourse has been about being impregnable. From a theological perspective, at the heart of the Christian narrative is the Incarnation, the embodiment of God in the person of Jesus, and with that comes the vulnerability of the flesh to crown of thorns, nails and spear, the physicality of washing feet and the feeding on bread and wine. Most of humanity's greatest crimes have been focused on bodies – of Jews, of people of colour, of women, of children and old people – and on what people do with their bodies, especially when touching and loving.

My wife is the voice coach at Ripon College Cuddesdon and I have enjoyed the many conversations we have had over the dinner table about posture, voice, breath and support, and presence. The way you talk and use your voice in leadership, whether in a small group or a large meeting, is crucially important. Often the first thing to suffer when you are under pressure is the voice. You are known as much by your voice as by your body and, as all voice coaches know, your voice is not only your larynx but is rooted deep in the very core of your body. Your voice holds and reveals who you are and how you feel about yourself, not only in your private life but also in the public sphere of your leadership.

Patsy Rodenburg,[10] an internationally known voice coach, writes about three circles of energy. In the first, called the Circle of Self and Withdrawal, you are focused on self, are not much available to the outside world, and tend to drain the energy out of other people. You will feel self-conscious, tend to wear clothes that help you to disappear and will find yourself holding your breath or breathing rapidly and shallowly. In the third circle, called the Circle of Bluff and Force, you are full of energy but it is sprayed everywhere and you make loose connections with the world. People notice that you are not very interested in them and you seem insensitive and overbearing. You will often seek to control every conversation, feel that you have to inject energy into every situation and wear clothes that will get you noticed, and your breath will be noisy. In the second circle, called the Circle of Connecting, you will be both giving and receiving energy because you are able to connect with other people and touch and influence them without impressing or imposing on them. You will feel that your body belongs to you, and your breath will be easy and free. Young children full of life are the best example of this circle.

So how you are in your body, staying connected physically to every part of yourself, is a crucial aspect of taking the strain of leadership. I was brought up to think of my body as the temple of the Holy Spirit, and while that laid many guilt trips on me as a teenager I think it is a perspective that has value. What we eat and drink and how we exercise and take recovery time are all very important.

There is a third aspect of taking the strain that is illuminated in the work of Edwin Friedman.[11] Friedman was an American rabbi, leader of a synagogue and also a family therapist. He noticed how often as a rabbi he got involved in congregational situations that felt just like the family processes he worked with as a therapist. Over and over again he found himself sucked into the emotional processes of the congregation, and he came to the conclusion that his job as a leader was to seek to define himself in such a way that he could separate himself from the seductive and collusive entrapment that was so common. Change came and was possible, he discovered, when he as leader could practise what he came to call self-differentiation. In many respects this is similar to the organizational analysis theories that I referred to earlier, and similar in practice to the work done by the Grubb Institute with its role analysis processes.

In working with families Friedman discovered that change came, not when he worked with the whole family, but when he could find the one family member who was most likely to self-differentiate and could work with that person. It is as if the dysfunctional system needs everyone to collude and play their part, but when one member stops 'playing the game' then healing and change can begin to happen.

> I began to concentrate on helping the leader to become better defined and to learn how to deal adroitly with the sabotage that almost invariably followed any success in this endeavor. Soon I found that the rest of the family was 'in therapy' whether or not they came into my office. For it is the integrity of the leader that

promotes the integrity or prevents the 'dis-integ-ration' of the system he or she is leading.[12]

In his leadership consultancy and training, Friedman found the same things to be true. He came to the conclusion that the emotional processes of society mingled with the emotional process of the organization and wove themselves into the emotional processes of the leader: 'I began to realize that before any technique or data could be effective, leaders had to be willing to face their own selves.'[13]

And in seeking to clarify what he meant by a well-differentiated leader he wrote:

> I do not mean an autocrat who tells others what to do or orders them around, although a leader who defines himself or herself clearly may be perceived that way by those who are not taking responsibility for their own emotional feeling and destiny. Rather, I mean someone who has clarity about his or her own life goals, and, therefore, someone who is less likely to become lost in the emotional processes swirling about. I mean someone who can be separate while still remaining connected, and therefore can maintain a modifying, non-anxious, and sometimes challenging presence. I mean someone who can manage their own reactivity to the automatic reactivity of others, and therefore be able to take stands at the risk of displeasing. It is not as though some leaders can do this and some cannot. No one does this easily, and most leaders, I have learned, can improve their capacity.[14]

Borrowing from the work of Richard Sennett[15] I want to suggest that leadership is a craft rather than a competence. The furniture maker or the musician and all craft workers develop an extraordinary ability to coordinate head and hand. This hand–head dialogue is formed and shaped by practice and the capacity for sustained attention, and develops the ability to recognize a problem and seek to solve it. It is out of this kind of thinking that we talk of a person having just the right kind of touch, even when referring to something like leadership. It may be a gift but it is of little use unless honed with hours and hours of practice. The craft worker learns from mistakes; is willing to take things to pieces and start again to find a more elegant solution; will pick the brains of fellow workers and try new ways of working. But there will be times of 'things not going well', and frustrations, and sometimes the learning will be slow and painful. 'Rome was not built in a day,' they say, and leadership as a craft is a lifetime's calling.

Jesus said that we should love the Lord our God with all our mind, heart, strength and soul, and it seems to me that we can take the strain and offer leadership in the Church and in the world when we allow God's love to shape and strengthen our minds, emotions, bodies and souls. This calling of Christ brings me to say something that is fundamental, and comes here because it is and needs to be a foundation of everything else that I have written. This is the disciplined practice of prayer. It may be in a quiet time, or the saying of a daily office or joining with others at a daily mass. This habit that we form and need to keep reforming reminds us of the vision and purposes of God for the world and for ourselves within it. It holds our intent and reshapes our perspective, which always gets out of shape. It restores us in relationship with eternal love. I know no one who finds this easy, or who is not tempted to give it up, and it is a daily temptation to me to pretend I can do without it.

It does not take long to write this, but it does take a lifetime of practice and struggle to find the deep strength to take the strain. The effort and the practice and the bruised hands and hearts are worth it.

Notes

An introduction

1 J. Adair (2005) *How to Grow Leaders: The seven key principles of effective leadership development* (Kogan Page, London) is one of many books John Adair has written and an excellent summary of much of his thinking.
2 See <www.grubb.org.uk>.
3 J. Micklethwait and A. Wooldridge (2009) *God is Back: How the global rise of faith is changing the world*, Allen Lane/Penguin, London.

1 Mapping the territory

1 S.R. Covey (1992) *The Seven Habits of Highly Effective People*, Simon & Schuster, London; S.R. Covey (2004) *The 8th Habit: From effectiveness to greatness*, Simon & Schuster, London.
2 J. Kotter (1996) *Leading Change*, Harvard Business School, Boston.
3 W. Bridges (2004) *Managing Transitions: Making sense of life's changes*, Da Capo Press, Cambridge, MA.
4 P. Senge (2005) *Presence: Exploring profound change in people, organisations and society*, Nicholas Brealey, London.
5 'Co-dependency' is a term used to describe the ways in which, for instance, a leader needs followers as much as followers need a leader. There grows between them a psychological contract that binds them together. The follower will end up excessively passive and the leader will end up excessively focused on the needs of the followers. For both leader and follower there develops a dysfunctional relationship between them that leaves both with low self-esteem. There is an excellent article in Wikipedia; see <en.wikipedia.org/wiki/codependency>.
6 J. Katzenbach (1998) *The Wisdom of Teams: Creating the high-performance organization*, McGraw Hill, London.
7 P. Lencioni (2002) *The Five Dysfunctions of a Team*, Jossey-Bass, San Francisco.

8 A. Dulles (1988) *Models of the Church: A critical assessment of the Church in all its aspects*, Gill & Macmillan, Dublin.

9 G. Morgan (1986) *Images of Organisation*, Sage, London.

10 S. Western (2008) *Leadership: A critical text*, Sage, London.

11 A. Hirsch and L. Sweet (2006) *The Forgotten Ways: Reactivating the missional Church*, Brazos, Ada, MI.

12 J. Collins and J. Porras (2005) *Built to Last: Successful habits of visionary companies*, Random House, London.

13 W. George (2007) *True North: Discover your authentic leadership*, Jossey-Bass, San Francisco.

14 W. Bennis (2010) *Still Surprised: A memoir to life in leadership*, Jossey-Bass, San Francisco.

15 Marcus Buckingham (2006) *The One Thing You Need to Know . . . about Great Managing, Great Leading and Sustained Individual Success*, Pocket Books, London.

16 C. Huffington (ed.) (2004) *Working below the Surface: The emotional life of contemporary organisations*, Tavistock Press, London.

17 Buckingham, *The One Thing You Need to Know*.

2 All leaders do it

1 P. Senge (1999) *The Dance of Change*, Nicholas Brealey, London.

2 R. Skynner (1990) *Institutes and How to Survive Them: Mental health training and consultation*, Routledge, London.

3 <www.americanrhetoric.com/speeches/mlkihaveadream.htm>.

4 <www.bristol.anglican.org/ministry/strategy/downloads/RTE%20 Strategy%20Overview.pdf>.

5 J. Collins (2005) *Good to Great and the Social Sectors*, Random House, London.

6 S. Hauerwas (2001) *The Hauerwas Reader*, Duke University Press, London.

7 Riazat Butt, 'Catholic defectors will leave Anglicans breathing sigh of relief – bishop', *Guardian*, 21 April 2011.

8 J. Collins (2001) *Good to Great*, Random House, London.

3 The monarch

1 J. Micklethwait and A. Wooldridge (2009) *God is Back: How the global rise of faith is changing the world*, Allen Lane/Penguin, London.

2 William Countryman (1999) *Living on the Border of the Holy: Renewing the priesthood of all*, Morehouse, Harrisburg, PA.

3 J.L. Badaracco, Jr (2006) *Questions of Character: Illuminating the heart of leadership*, HBS, Boston.

4 J. Collins (2005) *Good to Great and the Social Sectors*, HarperCollins, London.

5 J.G. Williams (ed.) (2000) *The Girard Reader*, Crossroad Herder, New York.

6 I. McGilchrist (2009) *The Master and His Emissary: The divided brain and the making of the Western world*, Yale University Press, London.

7 W.R. Bion (1961) *Experiences in Groups*, Tavistock Press, London.

8 E.J. Miller and A.K. Rice (1967) *Systems of Organisation: The control of task and sentient boundaries*, Tavistock Press, London.

9 I. Menzies Lyth (1959) 'The functions of social systems as a defence against anxiety: a report on a study of the nursing service in a general hospital', reprinted in I. Menzies Lyth (1988) *Selected Essays Volume 1: Containing anxiety in institutions*, Free Association Books, London.

10 B.D. Reed (1978) *Dynamics of Religion: Process and movement in Christian churches*, DLT, London.

11 W. Carr (1997) *Handbook of Pastoral Studies*, SPCK, London.

12 L. Hirschhorn (1990) *The Workplace Within: Psychodynamics of organizational life*, MIT Press, London; L. Hirschhorn (1997) *Reworking Authority: Leading and following in the post-modern organisation*, MIT Press, London.

13 I came across a quotation from Peter Drucker, reported in Micklethwait and Wooldridge, *God is Back*, in which he suggests that the large pastoral church (in the USA) has taken over from the company as the most significant organizational phenomenon. If this is true then the projections of dependency in church life continue and replace those of organizations.

14 W.A. Kraus (1980) *Collaboration in Organisations: Alternatives to hierarchy*, Human Sciences Press, New York/London.

15 See Youtube, RSA Animate Daniel Pink, <www.youtube.com/watch?v=u6XAPnuFjJc>.

16 For example, G. Hamel (2007) *The Future of Management*, HBS, Boston.

17 Ged Cray (2010) *New Monasticism as Fresh Expressions of Church*, Canterbury Press, Norwich; I. Adam (2010) *Cave, Refectory and Road*, Canterbury Press, Norwich.

18 An interesting counter-view is expressed in Deuteronomy 17.14–20.

4 The warrior

1 B. Hybels (2002) *Courageous Leadership*, Zondervan, Michigan.

2 B. Hybels (2008) *Axioms: Powerful leadership proverbs*, Zondervan, Michigan.

3 J. Micklethwait and A. Wooldridge (2009) *God is Back: How the global rise of faith is changing the world*, Allen Lane/Penguin, London, p. 81.

4 S. Western (2008) *Leadership: A critical text*, Sage, London.

5 An example here would be the work of Walter Wink with his book on principalities and powers (*The Powers that Be: Theology for a new millennium*, Doubleday, New York, 1998) or the revolutionary celebration of the mass before burning draft papers in the Vietnam War by Dan Berrigan (see Chapter 8).

6 H. Segal (1973) *An Introduction to the Work of Melanie Klein*, Karnac, London.

7 R. Howard (1996) *The Rise and Fall of the Nine O'Clock Service: A cult within the Church?* Mowbray, London.

8 Western, *Leadership*, p. 156.

9 A. Kahane (2004) *Solving Tough Problems*, Berrett-Koehler, San Francisco.

10 W.G. Lawrence (2000) *Tongued with Fire: Groups in experience*, Karnac, London.

11 R. Sennett (2006) *The Culture of the New Capitalism*, Yale University Press, London/New Haven, CT, p. 56.

5 The servant

1 R. Greenleaf (2002) *Servant Leadership (25ᵗʰ Anniversary Edition)*, Foreword by Stephen Covey and Afterword by Peter Senge, Paulist Press, Mahwah, NJ.

2 See <www.greenleaf.org>.

3 H. Hesse (2001) *The Journey to the East*, Peter Owen, London (first published 1956).

4 S. Rowland Jones (ed.) (2008) *Faith in Action*, Lux Verbi BM, Cape Town.

5 Mike D. Williams, second edition of training material, July 2001.

6 R. Dale (1986) *Pastoral Leadership*, Abingdon, Nashville, TN.

7 Afterword in Greenleaf, *Servant Leadership*.

8 J. Niewold (2007) 'Beyond servant leadership', *Journal of Biblical Persectives in Leadership*, Vol. 1, No. 2, Summer 2007, pp. 118–34.

9 M. Vasey (1995) *Strangers and Friends*, Hodder & Stoughton, London.

10 Liz Carmichael (2004) *Friendship: Interpreting Christian love*, T. & T. Clark, Edinburgh.

11 S. Pickard (2009) *Theological Foundations for Collaborative Ministry*, Ashgate, Farnham.

6 The elder

1 M. Sadgrove (2008) *Wisdom and Ministry: The call to leadership*, SPCK, London.

2 Plato, *The Republic*, 473, c–d.

3 V. Donovan (1978) *Christianity Rediscovered*, SCM Press, London.

4 T. Zeldin (1998) *Conversations*, Harvill, London.

5 Michael DeLashmutt, 'Guest editorial', *Theology*, Vol. 114, No. 3, May/June 2011, pp. 161–2.

6 R. Revans (1980) *Action Learning: New techniques for management*, Blond & Briggs, London.

7 W. Bennis (2010) *Still Surprised: A memoir of a life in leadership*, Jossey-Bass, San Francisco.

8 S. Cottrell (2009) *The Things He Said: The story of the first Easter Sunday*, SPCK, London.

9 See <http://qfp.quakerweb.org.uk/qfp1-02.html>.

7 The contemplative

1 This translation is by Dani Munoz, the chaplain at Los Olivos, a Spanish retreat house; <www.haciendalosolivos.org/>.

2 H.J.M. Nouwen (1989) *In the Name of Jesus: Reflections on Christian leadership*, DLT, London.

3 Nouwen, *In the Name of Jesus*, p. 17.

8 The prophet

1 D. Berrigan (1973) *America is Hard to Find*, SPCK, London.

2 G.A. Arbuckle (1993) *Refounding the Church: Dissent for leadership*, Geoffrey Chapman, London.

3 Arbuckle, *Refounding the Church*, p. 9.

4 Anon (2001) *The Cloud of Unknowing and Other Works*, Penguin Classics, London.

5 W.G. Lawrence (1998) *Social Dreaming @ Work*, Karnac, London.

6 D. Armstrong (2005) *Organisation in the Mind: Psychoanalysis, group relations and organisational consultancy*, Karnac, London.

9 Taking the strain

1 E.H. Peterson (1992) *Under the Unpredictable Plant: An exploration into vocational holiness*, Greenwing, London.

2 M. Cohen (1996) *The Divided Self: Closing the gap between belief and behaviour*, Marshall Pickering, London.

3 N. and T. Ormerod (1995) *When Ministers Sin: Sexual abuse in the churches*, Millennium Books, Newtown, NSW, Australia; P. Rutter (1990) *Sex in the Forbidden Zone*, Unwin, London.

4 R. Skynner (1990) *Institutes and How to Survive Them: Mental health training and consultation*, Routledge, London.

5 D. Goleman, R. Boyatzis and A. McKee (2002) *The New Leaders, Transforming the art of leadership into the science of results*, Little, Brown, London; R. Boyatzis and A. McKee (2005) *Resonant Leadership*, HBS, Boston.

6 R.M. Young (1994) *Mental Space*, Process Press, London, pp. 34, 52.

7 J. Groppel (2000) *The Corporate Athlete*, John Wiley, New York.

8 S.R. Covey (1992) *Seven Habits of Highly Effective People*, Simon & Schuster, London.

9 A. Sinclair (2007) *Leadership for the Disillusioned: Moving beyond myths and heroes to leading that liberates*, Allen and Unwin, Crows Nest, NSW, Australia.

10 P. Rodenburg (2007) *Presence: How to use positive energy for success in every situation*, Penguin, London.

11 E.H. Friedman (1985) *Generation to Generation: Family process in church and synagogue*, Guilford Press, London; E.H. Friedman (1999) *A Failure of Nerve: Leadership in the age of the quick fix*, Seabury, New York.

12 Friedman, *A Failure of Nerve*, p. 19.

13 Friedman, *A Failure of Nerve*, p. 21.

14 Friedman, *A Failure of Nerve*, p. 14.

15 R. Sennett (2008) *The Craftsman*, Allen Lane/Penguin, London.

Bibliography

Adair, J. (2002) *Inspiring Leadership*, Thorogood, London.

Adair, J. (ed.) (2004) *Creative Church Leadership*, Canterbury Press, Norwich.

Adair, J. (2005) *How to Grow Leaders: The seven key principles of effective leadership development*, Kogan Page, London.

Adam, I. (2010) *Cave, Refectory and Road*, Canterbury Press, Norwich.

Arbuckle, G.A. (1993) *Refounding the Church: Dissent for leadership*, Geoffrey Chapman, London.

Armstrong, D. (2005) *Organisation in the Mind: Psychoanalysis, group relations and organisational consultancy*, Karnac, London.

Badaracco, J.L., Jr (2006) *Questions of Character: Illuminating the heart of leadership*, HBS, Boston.

Beach, N. (2008) *Gifted to Lead: The art of leading as a woman in the Church*, Zondervan, Grand Rapids, MI.

Bennis, W. (1999) *Old Dogs, New Tricks: On creative and collaborative leadership*, Kogan Page, London.

Bennis, W. (2010) *Still Surprised: A memoir to life in leadership*, Jossey-Bass, San Francisco.

Berrigan, D. (1973) *America is Hard to Find*, SPCK, London.

Bion, W.R. (1961) *Experiences in Groups*, Tavistock Press, London.

Blanchard, K. (1999) *The Heart of a Leader: Insights on the art of influence*, Eagle Press, Guildford.

Blanchard, K. (2007) *Leading at a Higher Level*, Prentice Hall, London.

Boyatzis, R. and McKee, A. (2005) *Resonant Leadership*, HBS, Boston.

Bridges, W. (2004) *Managing Transitions: Making sense of life's changes*, Da Capo Press, Cambridge, MA.

Bridges, W. (2009) *Managing Transitions: Making the most of change*, Nicholas Brealey, London.

Buckingham, M. (2006) *The One Thing You Need to Know . . . about Great Managing, Great Leading and Sustained Individual Success*, Pocket Books, London.

Buckingham, M. and Clifton, D. (2002) *Now, Discover Your Strengths*, Simon & Schuster, London.

Butt, Riazat, 'Catholic defectors will leave Anglicans breathing sigh of relief – bishop', *Guardian*, 21 April 2011.

Carmichael, Liz (2004) *Friendship: Interpreting Christian love*, T. & T. Clark, Edinburgh.

Carr, W. (1997) *Handbook of Pastoral Studies*, SPCK, London.

Cohen, M. (1996) *The Divided Self: Closing the gap between belief and behaviour*, Marshall Pickering, London.

Collins, J. (2001) *Good to Great: Why some companies make the leap . . . and others don't*, Random House, London.

Collins, J. (2005) *Good to Great and the Social Sectors: Why business thinking is not the answer*, Random House, London.

Collins, J. (2009) *How the Mighty Fall and Why Some Companies Never Give In*, Random House, London.

Collins, J. and Porras, J.I. (2005) *Built to Last: Successful habits of visionary companies*, Random House, London.

Cottrell, S. (2008) *Hit the Ground Kneeling: Seeing leadership differently*, CHP, London.

Cottrell, S. (2009) *The Things He Said: The story of the first Easter Sunday*, SPCK, London.

Countryman, L.W. (1999) *Living on the Border of the Holy: Renewing the priesthood of all*, Morehouse, Harrisburg, PA.

Covey, S.R. (1992) *The Seven Habits of Highly Effective People*, Simon & Schuster, London.

Covey, S.R. (2004) *The 8th Habit: From effectiveness to greatness*, Simon & Schuster, London.

Covey, S.R. (2008) *The Speed of Trust: The one thing that changes everything*, Free Press, London.

Cray, G. (ed.) (2010) *New Monasticism as Fresh Expressions of Church*, Canterbury Press, Norwich.

Dale, R. (1986) *Pastoral Leadership*, Abingdon, Nashville, TN.

Davies, M. and Dodds, G. (2011) *Leadership in the Church for a People of Hope*, T. & T. Clark, London.

De Board, R. (1978) *The Psychoanalysis of Organisations*, Routledge, London.

DeLashmutt, M., 'Guest Editorial', *Theology*, Vol. 114, No. 3, May/June 2011, pp. 161–2.

Donovan, V. (1978) *Christianity Rediscovered*, SCM Press, London.

Dulles, A. (1988) *Models of the Church: A critical assessment of the Church in all its aspects*, Gill & Macmillan, Dublin.

Friedman, E.H. (1985) *Generation to Generation: Family process in church and synagogue*, Guilford Press, London.

Friedman, E.H. (1999) *A Failure of Nerve: Leadership in the age of the quick fix*, Seabury, New York.

George, W. (2007) *True North: Discover your authentic leadership*, Jossey-Bass, San Francisco.

Gill, R. and Burke, D. (1996) *Strategic Church Leadership*, SPCK, London.

Goleman, D. (1988) *Working with Emotional Intelligence*, Bloomsbury, London.

Goleman, D., Boyatzis, R. and McKee A. (2002) *The New Leaders: Transforming the art of leadership into the science of results*, Little, Brown, London.

Greenleaf, R. (1996) *On Becoming a Servant Leader*, Jossey-Bass, San Francisco.

Greenleaf, R. (1996) *Seeker and Servant: Reflections on religious leadership*, Jossey-Bass, San Francisco.

Greenleaf, R. (2002) *Servant Leadership (25th Anniversary Edition)*, Foreword by Stephen Covey and Afterword by Peter Senge, Paulist Press, Mahwah, NJ.

Greenleaf, R. (2003) *The Servant Leader Within: A transformative path*, Paulist Press, Mahwah, NJ.

Groppel, J. (2000) *The Corporate Athlete*, John Wiley, New York.

Hamel, G. (2007) *The Future of Management*, HBS, Boston.

Hauerwas, S. (2001) *The Hauerwas Reader*, Duke University Press, London.

Herrick, V. and Mann, I. (1998) *Jesus Wept: Reflections on vulnerability in leadership*, DLT, London.

Hesse, H. (2001) *The Journey to the East*, Peter Owen, London (first published 1956).

Higginson, R. (1996) *Transforming Leadership: A Christian approach to management*, SPCK, London.

Hirsch, A. and Sweet, L. (2006) *The Forgotten Ways: Reactivating the missional church*, Brazos Press, Ada, MI.

Hirschhorn, L. (1990) *The Workplace Within: Psychodynamics of organizational life*, MIT Press, London.

Hirschhorn, L. (1997) *Reworking Authority: Leading and following in the post-modern organization*, MIT Press, London.

Howard, R. (1996) *The Rise and Fall of the Nine O'Clock Service: A cult within the Church?* Mowbray, London.

Huffington, C. (ed.) (2004) *Working below the Surface: The emotional life of contemporary organisations*, Tavistock Press, London.

Hybels, B. (2002) *Courageous Leadership*, Zondervan, Grand Rapids, MI.

Hybels, B. (2008) *Axioms: Powerful leadership proverbs*, Zondervan, Grand Rapids, MI.

Jamieson, P. (1997) *Living at the Edge: Sacrament and solidarity in leadership*, Mowbray, London.

Kahane, A. (2004) *Solving Tough Problems*, Berrett-Koehler, San Francisco.

Katzenbach, J. (1998) *The Wisdom of Teams: Creating high-performance organisation*, McGraw Hill, London.

Kotter, J. (1996) *Leading Change*, Harvard Business School, Boston.

Kraus, W.A. (1980) *Collaboration in Organisations: Alternatives to hierarchy*, Human Sciences Press, New York/London.

Lawrence, J. (2004) *Growing Leaders*, BRF, Abingdon.

Lawrence, W.G. (1998) *Social Dreaming @ Work*, Karnac, London.

Lawrence, W.G. (2000) *Tongued with Fire: Groups in experience*, Karnac, London.

Lawrence, W.G. (2003) *Experiences in Social Dreaming*, Karnac, London.

Lencioni, P. (2002) *The Five Dysfunctions of a Team*, Jossey-Bass, San Francisco.

McGilchrist, I. (2009) *The Master and His Emissary: The divided brain and the making of the Western world*, Yale University Press, London.

Malphurs, A. (2003) *Being Leaders: The nature of authentic Christian leadership*, Baker, Grand Rapids, MI.

Maxwell, J. (2007) *The 21 Irrefutable Laws of Leadership*, Thomas Nelson, Dallas, TX.

Menzies Lyth, I. (1959) 'The functions of social systems as a defence against anxiety, a report on a study of the nursing service in a general hospital', reprinted in I. Menzies Lyth (1988) *Selected Essays*

Volume 1: Containing anxiety in institutions, Free Association Books, London.

Micklethwait, J. and Wooldridge, A. (2009) *God is Back: How the global rise of faith is changing the world*, Allen Lane/Penguin, London.

Miller, E. (1993) *From Dependency to Autonomy: Studies in organisations*, Free Association Press, London.

Miller, E.J. and Rice, A.K. (1967) *Systems of Organisation: The control of task and sentient boundaries*, Tavistock Press, London.

Morgan, G. (1986) *Images of Organisation*, Sage, London.

Nelson, J. (ed.) (1999) *Leading, Managing, Ministering*, Canterbury Press, Norwich.

Nelson, J. (ed.) (2008) *How to Become a Creative Church Leader*, Canterbury Press. London.

Niewold, J. (2007) 'Beyond servant leadership', *Journal of Biblical Perspectives in Leadership*, Vol. 1, No. 2, Summer 2007, pp. 118–34.

Nouwen, H.J.M. (1989) *In the Name of Jesus: Reflections on Christian leadership*, DLT, London.

Obholzer, A. (ed.) (1994) *The Unconscious at Work: Individual and organisational stress in the human services*, Routledge, London.

Ormerod, N. and T. (1995) *When Ministers Sin: Sexual abuse in the churches*, Millennium Books, Newtown, NSW, Australia.

Patching, K. (2007) *Leadership, Character and Strategy: Exploring diversity*, Palgrave Macmillan, Basingstoke.

Peterson, E.H. (1992) *Under the Unpredictable Plant: An exploration into vocational holiness*, Greenwing, London.

Pickard, S. (2009) *Theological Foundations for Collaborative Ministry*, Ashgate, Farnham.

Quinn, R. (1996) *Deep Change: Discovering the leader within*, Jossey-Bass, San Francisco.

Quinn, R. (2004) *Building the Bridge as You Walk on it: A guide for leading change*, Jossey-Bass, San Francisco.

Read, B.D. (1978) *Dynamics of Religion: Process and movement in Christian churches*, DLT, London.

Revans, R. (1980) *Action Learning: New techniques for management*, Blond & Briggs, London.

Rodenburg, P. (2007) *Presence: How to use positive energy for success in every situation*, Penguin, London.

Rowland Jones, S. (ed.) (2008) *Faith in Action*, Lux Verbi BM, Cape Town.

Rutter, P. (1990) *Sex in the Forbidden Zone*, Unwin, London.

Sadgrove, M. (2008) *Wisdom and Ministry: The call to leadership*, SPCK, London.

Segal, H. (1973) *An Introduction to the Work of Melanie Klein*, Karnac, London.

Senge, P. (1999) *The Dance of Change*, Nicholas Brealey, London.

Senge, P. (2005) *Presence: Exploring profound change in people, organisations and society*, Nicholas Brealey, London.

Sennett, R. (2006) *The Culture of the New Capitalism*, Yale University Press, London/New Haven, CT.

Sennett, R. (2008) *The Craftsman*, Allen Lane/Penguin, London.

Shaw, P. (2004) *Mirroring Jesus as Leader*, Grove Books, Cambridge.

Sinclair, A. (2007) *Leadership for the Disillusioned: Moving beyond myths and heroes to leading that liberates*, Allen and Unwin, Crows Nest, NSW, Australia.

Sipe, J. and Frick, D. (2009) *Seven Pillars of Servant Leadership*, Paulist Press, Mahwah, NJ.

Skynner, R. (1990) *Institutes and How to Survive Them: Mental health training and consultation*, Routledge, London.

Stapley, L. (2006) *Individuals, Groups, and Organisations beneath the Surface*, Karnac, London.

Treston, K. (1997) *Creative Christian Leadership: Skills for more effective ministry*, Twenty-Third Publications, Mystic, CT.

Vasey, M. (1995) *Strangers and Friends*, Hodder & Stoughton, London.

Walker, S.P. (2007) *Leading Out of Who You Are*, Piquant Editions, Carlisle.

Ward, R. (2008) *Growing Women Leaders*, Bible Reading Fellowship, Abingdon.

Western, S. (2008) *Leadership: A critical text*, Sage, London.

Wheatley, M. (1999) *Leadership and the New Science*, Berrett-Koehler, San Francisco.

Williams, J.G. (ed.) (2000) *The Girard Reader*, Crossroad Herder, New York.

Wink, W. (1998) *The Powers that Be: Theology for a new millennium*, Doubleday, New York.

Wright, W.C. (2000) *Relational Leadership*, Paternoster Press, Milton Keynes.

Wright, W.C. (2005) *Don't Step on the Rope: Reflections on leadership, relationships and teamwork*, Paternoster Press, Milton Keynes.

Young, R.M. (1994) *Mental Space*, Process Press, London.

Zaragoza, E. (1999) *No Longer Servants, but Friends: A theology of ordained ministry*, Abingdon, Nashville, TN.

Zeldin, T. (1998) *Conversation: How talk can change your life*, Harvill, London.

Index

22479306R00072

Printed in Great Britain
by Amazon